Purchased with funds
provided by
Friends of the Jacksonville Library

JACKSON COUNTY
Library Services

NATIVE TRIBES OF THE
PLAINS AND PRAIRIE

Michael Johnson

Please visit our web site at: **www.worldalmanaclibrary.com**
For a free color catalog describing World Almanac® Library's list
of high-quality books and multimedia programs, call 1-800-848-2928 (USA)
or 1-800-387-3178 (Canada). World Almanac® Library's fax: (414) 332-3567.

Library of Congress Cataloging-in-Publication Data

Johnson, Michael, 1937 Apr. 22-
    Native tribes of the Plains and prairie / by Michael Johnson.
      p. cm.— (Native tribes of North America)
    Summary: An introduction to the history, culture, and people of the many Indian tribes that inhabited the region between the Mississippi River
and the Rocky Mountains, including the present Prairie provinces of Canada.
    Includes bibliographical references and index.
    ISBN 0-8368-5613-9 (lib. bdg.)
    1. Indians of North America—Great Plains—History—Juvenile literature. 2. Indians of North America—Prairie Provinces—History—Juvenile literature.
3. Indians of North America—Great Plains—Social life and customs—Juvenile literature. 4. Indians of North America—Prairie Provinces—Social life and
customs—Juvenile literature. [1. Indians of North America—Great Plains. 2. Indians of North America—Prairie Provinces.] I. Title.
E78.G73J594 2004
978.004'97—dc22
                                                2003060595

This North American edition first published in 2004 by
World Almanac® Library
330 West Olive Street, Suite 100
Milwaukee, WI 53212 USA

For Compendium Publishing
Contributor: Michael Johnson
Editor: Michael Burke
Picture research: Michael Johnson and Simon Forty
Design: Tony Stocks/Compendium Design
Maps: Mark Franklin

World Almanac® Library editor: Gini Holland
World Almanac® Library graphic designer: Steve Schraenkler

Picture credits
All artwork (other than maps) reproduced by kind permission of Richard Hook. All photographs are by Michael Johnson or supplied from his
collection unless credited otherwise below. Particular thanks are due to the staff of Royal Albert Memorial Museum and Art Gallery, Exeter,
Devon, U.K., for assistance and access to its exhibits, archives, and excellent collections, and to Bill Yenne for material of his own and from his
collection. Much of the material in this book appeared as part of *The Encyclopedia of Native Tribes of North America* by M. J. Johnson and
R. Hook, published by Compendium Publishing Ltd. in 2001.

Cambridge University Museum of Archaeology & Anthropology, U.K.: pp. 23 (left); Harry Pollard Collection, Provincial Museum & Archives of Alberta,
Edmonton: pp. 17, 19 (below), 20; Linden Museum, Stuttgart: p. 37; Richard Green Collection (photography by Simon Clay): pp. 8 (right), 9, 12 (right), 24, 29
(below), 43 (above), 44 (above), 47 (below), 48; Royal Albert Memorial Museum and Art Gallery: pp. 1, 51; Southern Plains Indian Museum, Anadarko,
Oklahoma: p. 34 (right); Courtesy Ian West: p. 16 (Glacier Studio), p. 33 (Montana Historical Society), 34 (left/Soule Photos); Courtesy Ray Whiteway-Roberts:
p. 31 (below).

Printed in the United States of America

1 2 3 4 5 6 7 8 9 08 07 06 05 04

Cover: Chief Plenty Coups, Crow Indian, Montana, c. 1910. He wears a typical Crow shirt and an eagle feather headdress with ermine skin drops, often
known as a "war bonnet." A headdress belonging to Chief Plenty Coups is on display at the National Cemetery, Arlington, Virginia.

Previous Page: Blackfoot man's skin shirt, leggings, and moccasins. The shirt is a classic mid-nineteenth century chief's shirt, of two large deer skins, the
bottom two-thirds of each forming the front and back. The remaining skins form the two sleeves. The shirt is decorated with beaded strips, large chest
discs, painted stripes, and hairlock fringes.

Contents

Introduction

For thousands of years, the people known today as Native Americans or American Indians have inhabited the whole of the Americas, from Alaska to the southernmost tip of South America. Most scholars and anthropologists think that the ancestors of Native peoples came to the Americas from Asia over a land mass connecting Siberia and Alaska. These first Americans may have arrived as long as 30,000 years ago, although most historians estimate that this migration took place 15,000 years ago.

According to this theory, Paleo-Indians (*paleo*, from a Greek word meaning "ancient") migrated over many years down through an ice-free corridor in North America, spreading out from west to east and southward into Central and South America. In time, they inhabited the entire Western Hemisphere from north to south. Their descendants became the many diverse Native peoples encountered by European explorers and settlers.

"INDIANS" VS. "NATIVE AMERICANS"

Christopher Columbus is said to have "discovered" the Americas in 1492. But did he? Columbus was not the first European to visit what became known as the New World; Viking mariners had sailed to Greenland and Newfoundland almost five hundred years before and even founded short-lived colonies. Using the word "discovered" also ignores the fact that North America was already inhabited by Native civilizations whose ancestors had "discovered" the Americas for themselves.

When Columbus landed on an island he called San Salvador (Spanish for "Holy Savior"), he thought he had reached China or Japan. He had sailed west intending to get to the East—to Asia, or the fabled "Indies," as it was often called by Europeans of the time. Although he landed in the Bahamas, Columbus never really gave up on the idea that he had made it to the Indies. Thus, when Native people first encountered Columbus and his men in the islands off Florida, the lost explorer called them "Indians." The original names that each tribal group had already given to themselves usually translate into English as "the people" or "human beings." Today, some Native people of North

Above: **Assiniboine warrior with buffalo robe, gun, and wearing a porcupine quillwork decorated shirt. Painting by Karl Bodmer, 1833, at Fort Union, on the upper Missouri River.**

America prefer to be called "American Indians," while others prefer "Native Americans." In this book, Native peoples will be referred to by their tribal names or, in more general cases, as "Indians".

Today's Indians are descended from cultures of great historical depth, diversity, and complexity. Their ancient ancestors, the Paleo-Indians, developed beliefs and behavior patterns that enabled them to survive in unpredictable and often harsh environments. These early hunter-gatherers had a close relationship with the land and a sense of absolute and eternal belonging to it. To them, everything in their world—trees, mountains, rivers, sky, animals, rock formations—had "spirit power," which they respected and placated through prayers and rituals in order to ensure their survival. These beliefs evolved over time into a fascinating and diverse series of creation stories, trickster tales, songs, prayers, and rituals passed down to and practiced by tribes throughout North America. Although many Indians today practice Christianity and other religions as well, many of their traditional songs, stories, dances, and other practices survive, on reservations and in areas where substantial tribal groups still live.

A CONTINENT OF CULTURES

Long before the Europeans arrived, important Indian cultures had already developed and disappeared. The ancient Adena and Hopewell people, for example, built a number of extraordinary burial mounds, and later even large towns, some of whose remains can still be seen at sites in the Midwest and South. These cultures were themselves gradually influenced by Mesoamerican (pre-Columbian Mexican and Central American) farming cultures based on growing maize (Indian corn), beans, and squash. They became the Mississippian culture from 700 A.D. The great spread of language groups across the North American continent also points to a rich Indian history of continual movement, invasion, migration, and conquest that took place long before European contact.

By the time the first European explorers and colonists set foot in North America, Indians had settled across the vast continent into different tribal groups and cultures that were active, energetic, and continually changing. American Indians were skilled in exploiting their particular

U.S. INDIAN POPULATION

There is no record of the number of Indians living north of the Rio Grande before Europeans came. A conservative estimate of Indian population made by ethnographer James Mooney is about 1,250,000 for the late sixteenth century, before the founding of Jamestown and Plymouth. Others have suggested figures as high as six million, although two to three million might be more realistic. The highest concentrations of people were in the coastal regions: the Atlantic slope in the East, along the Gulf of Mexico in the South, and in California in the West. Indians living in these areas also suffered the most from European diseases, and from conflict with European colonists. Population figures for the twentieth century vary considerably, due mainly to U.S. government criteria used to determine who is or is not an Indian. Also, the U.S. Bureau of Indian Affairs (BIA), the official bureaucracy in charge of the remaining Indian lands and federal services to Indians, has few relations with Indians in certain states. Thus the BIA's population figures tend to be lower than those reported by the U.S. Census. In 1950, the BIA reported 396,000 enrolled Indians, of whom 245,000 were resident on reservations. The U.S. Census reported 827,108 Indians in 1970 and 1,418,195 in 1980. Census 2000 recorded 2,409,578 respondents who reported as American Indian or Alaskan Native only and identified a single tribe of origin.

Above: **The Prairie was once teeming with life—buffalo, antelope, and deer—and the Native Americans made full use of it for sustenance, clothing, and all manner of tools and equipment.**

Above right: **The Plains and Prairies area covered by this book stretches from the Mississippi Valley to the Rocky Mountains.**

environments in a multitude of ways developed over time. They were also good at incorporating new methods and technologies from other peoples. When Europeans came, many Indians adapted European technology to their own way of life, incorporating, for example, the horse, the rifle, money, beads, fabric, steel implements, and European-style agriculture into their own traditional cultures. In many cases, however, the benefits of European influence were eventually overshadowed by the displacement or outright destruction of traditional Native life.

WHAT THIS BOOK COVERS

The purpose of this book is to give some relevant facts about the main tribes native to the Plains and Prairie. Included here are brief historical sketches of the tribes, descriptions of tribal language relationships and groups, and accounts of traditional cultures, tribal locations, and populations in early and recent times. Interaction with invading Europeans is shown in discussions of trade, wars, treaties, and the eventual Indian removal to lands whose boundaries served more to keep Indians in than to keep white settlers out. Today's political boundaries were not recognized by Indians on their original lands; their "borders" were defined by shifting areas of hunting, gathering, and farming that Native groups used and fought over. For ease of reference, however, tribal locations given here refer to modern U.S. and Canadian place names.

THE PLAINS AND PRAIRIE

The Indian tribes of the Plains and Prairie cultural area ranged from the Mississippi Valley in the east to the Rocky Mountains of the west and all the way from the Saskatchewan River in Canada to the Rio Grande bordering Mexico. The dry western High Plains were covered with short grass, while the dark soil and wetter climate of the east supported tall prairie grasses. The main river systems run west to east and link the Missouri and the Mississippi, with forested patches between these rivers. The area once teemed with animals—buffalo (bison), pronghorn antelope, wolves, coyotes, deer, and bears.

The arrival of the horse changed the way of life of the High Plains peoples significantly. From the seventeenth century onward, other changes included the arrival of the

Plains & Prairie

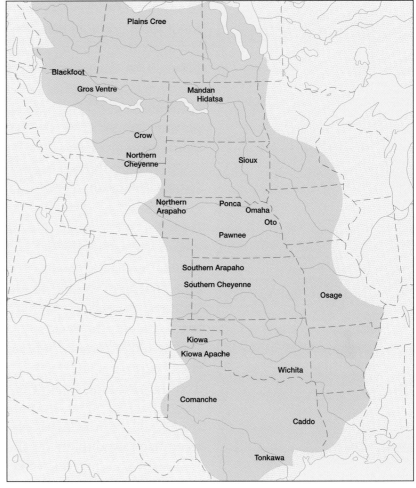

Plains Cree

Blackfoot

Gros Ventre

Mandan
Hidatsa

Crow

Northern
Cheyenne

Sioux

Northern
Arapaho

Ponca

Omaha

Oto

Pawnee

Southern Arapaho

Southern Cheyenne

Osage

Kiowa

Kiowa Apache

Wichita

Comanche

Caddo

Tonkawa

gun, the growth of the European fur trade, and the exchange of trade goods.

The way of life of the nomadic High Plains peoples depended almost entirely on the bison: The parts of the animal they did not eat they used to make robes, tipis, and artifacts. Otherwise, they ate roots and berries and a little fish, but they were not farmers. They made clothing from animal skins, often from members of the deer family including wapiti (Shawnee for "white rump" elk), elk, pronghorn antelope, big horn sheep, and moose in the far north. Plains clothing and rawhide containers were often decorated with geometric art. The *travois,* made of two poles crossed in an A-shape with a platform on top and pulled by a dog or a horse, was their method of transport.

Plains Indian society was organized into tipi camp circles of related people or bands and religious societies. Religious practices included the Sun Dance, sweat lodge, and vision quest. The tribes that followed this nomadic way of life included the Blackfeet, Gros Ventre (or Atsina), Assiniboine, Crow, Sioux, Cheyenne, and Arapaho, all of whom entered the Plains from the east; the Kiowa who entered from the north; and the Comanche, who split from the Shoshone.

The Prairie culture is much older. Here tribes lived in semipermanent earth lodge dwellings along the Missouri,

CENSUS 2000 FIGURES
Wherever possible U.S. Census 2000 figures are supplied with each entry showing the number of people who identified that they were American Indian or Alaskan Native and members of only one tribe. Other people reported as American Indian or Alaskan Native in combination with one or more other races (defined in the census as including white, black or African-American, Native Hawaiian, and other Pacific Islander) and showing more than one tribe of origin are identified as "part. . . ." Reporting variables mean that some of the totals published here may not be the precise sum of the individual elements.

Above: **The bison, or American buffalo—the staff of life for the Plains Indians. Before the horse arrived, some Plains Indian hunters would chase herds off of cliffs to claim their meat and hides.**

Right: **selection of Plains moccasins displaying an array of colorful beadwork designs.**

Republican, and Platte Rivers. They grew corn and ate meat from game in season. Tribes who lived this way included the Pawnee, Arikara, Hidatsa, Mandan, Omaha, Ponca, Oto, Missouri, and Osage. Typical Prairie culture elements were steatite (soapstone) sculptures for pipes, ceremonial and religious organizations, small effigy altar platforms, medicine bundles, and catlinite (pipestone) calumets, or "peace pipes."

Another influence came from the Rocky Mountain tribes—especially the Shoshone, Salish, and Sahaptian groups—whose mythology concentrated around the trickster and culture hero Coyote. On the edges of these were the Caddoan tribes in the southeastern regions, eastern groups such as the Cree and Ojibwa in the North, and Apachean groups in the Southwest. For over three hundred years these cultures intermingled, continually trading goods and ideas.

The old Prairie tribes belonged to two language families: the Siouan, a word derived from the Sioux (Dakota), and the Caddoan (from the southeastern Caddo or Kadohadacho). The Winnebago, a woodland people, were the Siouans left in the East as the Siouans gradually moved west, then north and south to occupy the river bottoms and raise beans, squash, tobacco, and corn. The Caddoans spread out from America's agricultural heartland; the Arikara followed the Siouan Mandan north; the Pawnee occupied the central Republican, Platte, and Missouri River areas; while the southern Caddoans were found in Kansas, Texas, Oklahoma, and Arkansas. The Wichita erected their grass-thatched lodges as far north as the Great Bend of the Arkansas (in modern Kansas).

The three Blackfeet tribes were the first Algonkian peoples to move north and west. Meanwhile, the most significant development was the appearance in the northern plains of the Sioux from the prairies and woods of Minnesota. The Western Sioux turned into nomadic Plains Indians, plundered the

Missouri village tribes, and pushed on ethnic groups who were on their way west, such as the Algonkian Arapaho, Gros Ventre, and Cheyenne (the latter had been a fairly settled group in the Prairie region).

The most important change to Plains culture by far was the introduction of horses from the Spanish colonies in the Southwest. The horse rapidly became essential to Indian life; allowing the people to become more mobile, carry more goods and larger tipis, and spread far more widely over the western plains. Originally a feared, mysterious, large animal, the horse eventually became revered. Horses probably came from the Spanish and Pueblos in the Santa Fe area to the Utes of the Great Basin by 1640, then to the Shoshone, then to the Plateau tribes and the Crow, and finally to the Blackfeet by about 1730. Also, they may have come from Santa Fe and San Antonio north to the Kiowa and Comanche, and finally to the Sioux. Horses were traded for corn and robes at the Mandan farming villages and from them to the Assiniboine, Cree, and Plains Ojibwa in exchange for European trade goods.

The Prairie tribes cultivated crops in season and hunted buffalo when they could. Their spiritual beliefs centered around hunting, and their ceremonies followed the seasons and social functions, notably the Calumet ritual, peace and war pipes, and rituals to guarantee a good corn harvest. The Pawnee, for example, believed in a high god, star and cosmological mythology, medicine bundles, and even human sacrifices to the Morning Star. They saw themselves as a mysterious part of the great cosmic structure which was covered by the dome of the sky, where lived the Supreme Being and supernatural star gods who used a great power known to the Sioux as *Wakan*.

Besides the significant group festivals—of which the Sun Dance and the Okeepa of the Missouri River village tribes stand out— warriors and individuals sought the help of animal spirits on their own, through visions brought on by fasting and dreaming. High Plains warriors

Above: **A Blackfeet tobacco bag and pipe.**

developed a range of age-graded military societies, each having its own chief. Other mystical organizations existed as well, such as dream societies that sought power from dreamed animals, often buffalo or elk, which they believed provided sexual power. In a time of despair following the loss of much of their culture in the nineteenth century, there appeared among the Plains tribes several religious movements, notably the Ghost Dance of the 1880s and 1890s and the Peyote religion—a mixture of Mexican Indian, Christian, and Plains Indian symbolism.

Plains warriors wore clothes that contained animal and bird elements linked to tracking, hunting, and battlefield trophies. Their clothing was decorated with geometric patterns and pictures. The Plains peoples were superb quillworkers and later beadworkers and decorated male and female dress with geometric designs, perhaps influenced in the late nineteenth century by imported Middle Eastern rugs. The beginning of the eighteenth century also saw the influx of other European trade goods—cloth, beads, metals, and guns—together with the spread of material culture from the Cree, Ojibwa, and Métis from Canada, which added greatly to the cultural mix of the entire Plains region.

THE SUN DANCE

The Sun Dance was the most important of all Plains Indian ceremonies (although it was not held by the Pawnee, Kiowa Apache, or Comanche). It is a re-creation ceremony of world renewal. The Plains Cree considered the dance an offering of thanks for the reawakening of nature after the silence of winter. They call it the "Thirsting Dance," because the dancers were forbidden to drink during its performance. The Cheyenne called the Sun Dance shelter "New Life Lodge" or "Lodge of New Birth." For them the ceremony re-creates, reshapes, and reanimates the earth and all its plants and animals while at the same time offering thanks to a Supreme Being.

The Sun Dance followed a set pattern. It started during winter when a man or woman made a vow to dance or felt a visionary command to do so. Secret rituals began in a tipi between the pledger and shamans (priests), usually older men who were experienced in the ceremony. These rituals purified those taking part and helped them learn the sacred songs and paint ritual designs. At the same time, an

Above: **Archie Eagle, Santee (Eastern) Sioux, White Cap Reserve, Saskatchewan. Photograph taken at Sioux Valley, Manitoba, 1972, by James H. Howard.**

Above right: **Participants in the Sun Dance on the Pine Ridge (Oglala Sioux) Reservation, South Dakota, c. 1964.**

important warrior or group of warriors killed a buffalo bull with one shot. Others looked for a forked tree which would be "killed" by a virtuous woman or captive and cut down. Both buffalo and tree were then taken to the Sun Dance site. Meanwhile, others set up a circle of ten to twenty posts, up to 20 yards (18 meters) in diameter, with an entrance to the east. The center pole had a bundle of brush near the top— the Thunderbird nest—as well as the head or skin of the killed buffalo and other objects, such as a Sun Dance doll (Blackfeet) or cloth offering. Rafters joined the posts to the center pole. The public second phase began with the formal procession of barefoot, kilt-clad, white-painted dancers into the lodge, taking their places on both sides of the altar. Looking constantly at the center pole or the sun, they would raise and lower their heels, bend their knees, and blow their eagle bone whistles at every drum beat. Dancing for several days and nights, they hoped to get a vision or at least to arouse the pity of a supernatural being.

In both the beginning and public phases of the rite (usually lasting four days), lesser ceremonies took place: male and female initiation into societies, curing of the sick, exhibitions of supernatural power, telling of warrior deeds, and distribution of wealth. Finally, among several tribes, some would have themselves skewered through their shoulder muscles to the center pole, dancing and hoping to gain supernatural aid through their painful sacrifice.

TRIBAL NAMES

Arapaho	trader	Osage	one who carries a message
Arikara or Ree	horns or elk	Oto or Otoe	lechers
Assiniboine and Stoney	one who cooks with hot stones	Pawnee	a horn
Blackfoot or Blackfeet	black moccasins	Ponca	sacred head
Cheyenne	red talkers	Quapaw	downstream people
Comanche	Spanish term	Sarsi	not good
Crow	bird people	Sioux or Dakota	little adders (Ojibwa)
Gros Ventre or Atsina	gut people		allies (Dakota)
Hidatsa or Minitaree	willows	Sisseton Sioux	swamp villagers
Iowa	sleepy ones	Tawakoni	neck of land in the water
Kansas	wind people	Teton Sioux	dwellers on the prairie
Kichai or Kitsai	going in wet sand or red shield	Waco	English name
		Wahpekute Sioux	leaf shooters
Kiowa	principal people	Wahpeton Sioux	dwellers in the leaves
Mandan	Dakota name	Wichita	big arbor
Mdewakanton Sioux	spirit lake dwellers	Yankton Sioux	dwellers at the end
Missouri	people with dugout canoes	Yanktonai Sioux	little dwellers at the end
Omaha	those going against the wind or current		

The Arapaho are survivors of an Algonkian-speaking tribe of the Plains who originated from the headwaters of the Mississippi River or perhaps from Canada. Less warlike than the Cheyenne, they were noted instead for their spiritual and religious manner. The Northern band still possesses the sacred pipe whose bearer formed the center of their camps in nomadic times. They were nomadic hunters of bison and developed an age-graded military society for males.

After crossing the Missouri River they pressed on to the headwaters of the Platte River and to the edge of the Rockies in present-day eastern Wyoming by 1820. By 1835, some of the tribe had moved south to the upper Arkansas River in eastern Colorado, thus forming the Northern and Southern branches of their tribe. At this time, they were in constant alliance with the Cheyenne but were often at war with the Shoshone, Ute, and Pawnee. They also raided with the Kiowa and Comanche, with whom they had friendly relations.

The Arapaho signed a treaty with the U.S. government in 1861, but the Southern branch and their allied Cheyenne suffered the Sand Creek Massacre of 1864 (where many were slain in spite of attempts at a peaceful surrender). A treaty signed at Medicine Lodge River in

Kansas in 1867 assigned them to lands in western Indian Territory (now Oklahoma), where their descendants remain, intermarried with the Cheyenne, mostly in Blaine and Washita counties, Oklahoma.

Assigned to the Wind River Reservation, Wyoming, the Northern Arapaho made peace with the Wind River Shoshone and now share the reservation. In pre-reservation days, the Arapaho numbered 3,000; in 1923, the Southern Arapaho were 833 and the Northern branch 921; in 1950, the Southern branch were 1,189; and in 1960, the Northern Arapaho were 2,279. In 1970, the combined population was 2,993 and in 1990 about 6,000. Many fought for the United States in World War II in the Pacific and Europe.

Above: **Clothing displayed inside an Arapaho or Cheyenne tipi.**

Far left: **An Arapaho wearing an eagle feather "war bonnet" and holding a tobacco bag and fan. Photograph taken by C. Carpenter, St. Louis Exposition, 1904.**

Left: **An Arapaho woman's richly beaded leggings, c. 1880.**

CENSUS 2000

The numbers recorded for the Arapaho were:

Arapaho	2,509
Northern Arapaho	4,410
Southern Arapaho	67
Wind River Arapaho	14
Total	7,000

TIPIS

The *tipi* is the conical lodge of the true High Plains nomads. They constructed them of buffalo hide erected on a framework of "lodge" poles. The tipi probably evolved from Subarctic prototypes; early forms were small, before the coming of the horse allowed transportation of larger covers and longer poles. Basic construction was fairly constant throughout the Plains: a tilted cone of straight, slim, peeled poles (usually lodgepole pine, cedar, or spruce) was slotted into a foundation frame of three or four poles. Foundation poles were usually tied together over the spread ground cover, then hoisted, the remaining poles being slotted into the crotches which they formed. In three-pole foundations, they faced one pole east and formed a door pole on the south side. Four-pole foundations formed a rectangle, the rear two remaining low at the back and appearing as a "swallow-tail" in the completed lodge. The tipi usually faced east toward the rising sun; being an imperfect cone, it had a back steeper than the front, which helped brace it against the wind. Covers were usually of dressed buffalo cow hides before the destruction of the herds in the 1880s and thereafter of traded canvas duck, usually white. Most nineteenth-century tipis were about 12-18 feet (4-5 m) high, requiring about a dozen skins sewn together and cut to a half-circle plan. Some covers and liners were painted with naturalistic or geometrical symbolic patterns, usually peculiar to the owner of the tipi and associated with the spiritual nature of the lodge.

The Assiniboine and the closely related Stoney are a large Siouan tribe who spoke a language similar to that of the Yanktonai (Dakota) Sioux, from whom they are believed to descend. They occupied an area between Lake Superior and James Bay, neighboring lands dominated by the Crees and the Hudson's Bay traders. It is thought that they slowly migrated westward in the early nineteenth century, in the course of which they split into two groups. In the north they settled from Moose Mountain along the South Saskatchewan and Qu'Appelle Rivers in Saskatchewan, and in the south they ranged to the Missouri River and in the west to the Cypress Hills.

The tribe lost many members to the ravages of smallpox during the nineteeenth century. This prompted a number of the Saskatchewan Assiniboine to move to the foothills of the Rocky Mountains; this group became known as "Stoney," apparently because of their method of cooking with hot stones. Assiniboine and Stoney culture was much the same as that of the Blackfeet during the nineteenth century but, like the

Cree, they developed a long association with white traders.

Those members who remained in Canada lived on several reserves. The Mosquito, Grizzly Bear's Head, and Lean Man's bands settled near Battleford, Saskatchewan. The Pheasant Rump's and Ocean Man's bands settled near Moose Mountain (later moved to the White Bear Reserve). The Carry-the-Kettle band settled at Fort Qu'Appelle; Joseph's and Paul's bands near Edmonton and Chiniquay, Alberta. The largest group, Wesley and Bearspaw, settled near Morley, Alberta.

In 1904, the Canadian Stoney and Assiniboine numbered 1,371. Those settled on two Montana reservations, Fort Peck and Fort Belknap, totaled 1,234, a huge reduction from an original population of perhaps 10,000. In 1970, in Saskatchewan, the Mosquito-Grizzly Bear's Head numbered 387, a few were at White Bear, and Carry-the-Kettle numbered 734; in Alberta, Alexis recorded 490, Paul's 575, and Chiniquay, Wesley, and Bearspaw (Stoney) 1,610; while 2,219 were divided almost equally between Fort Peck, where they were mixed with Yanktonai Sioux, and Fort Belknap, where they were mixed with Gros Ventre. In 1990, there were a reported 8,120 Assiniboine in the United States. Immortalized by the artists George Catlin and Karl Bodmer during the 1830s, after World War II they organized to regain their hunting rights. Today they use much of their oil and gas profits to promote their language and culture.

Above: **Assiniboine from Morley, Alberta, photographed at Banff Indian Days, c. 1950; second right is George Maclean (Walking Buffalo), who toured the world for the Moral Rearmament movement. Photograph: Nicolas Morant**

CENSUS 2000

The numbers recorded for the Assiniboine were:

Assiniboine	2,570
Fort Peck Assiniboine	302
Fort Belknap Assiniboine	1,074
Total	3,946

Above: **This superb portrait of Eagle Child illustrates some typical facial characteristics and dress of the Blackfeet. Note the flaring eagle feather bonnet, with white disks and horsehair trim at each feather tip, beaded brow band, and ermine drops, which replaced in popularity the "straight up" style during the late nineteenth century.**

A vibrant tribe today, the historic Blackfeet (U.S) or Blackfoot (Canadian), an Algonkian people, were a loose confederacy of three closely related tribes: the Blackfoot or North Blackfoot (Siksika), the Blood (Kainah), and Piegan(Pikuni)—spelled Peigan in Canada. They also enjoyed a close alliance with the Atsina (Gros Ventre) and Sarsi.

The Blackfeet once held an immense territory stretching from the North Saskatchewan River in Canada to the headwaters of the Missouri River in Montana, including the foothills of the Rocky Mountains. They seem to have moved from the East and were among the first Algonkians to relocate in the West after the arrival of Europeans. David Thompson, an explorer for the Hudson's Bay Company, made the first thorough European record of Blackfeet culture when he wintered with them in 1787–88; he found that they had owned horses, European guns, and metal objects for at least fifty years.

They seem to have been in conflict with the Snake Indians (probably Shoshone), whom they ultimately appear to have driven from the area. Despite the ravages of smallpox, particularly among the Piegans, the pre-reservation Blackfoot became the most powerful tribe of the northern Plains. They were a typical Plains tribe, depending on the buffalo for food, tipis, bedding, shields, clothing, and containers. They formed into age-related men's societies and formal religious group. The wealthy and fit members of each band looked after the young and old. Their religion used "bundles" that contained symbols—bits of animals, birds, and objects—which represented the power of dreamed or vision experiences and were used as a personal power source. These bundles were occasionally ceremoniously opened for group benefit, conferring health, good hunting, and prestige.

Below: **Pretty Young Man (Blackfoot name Ma-Ko-Yo-Mah-Kan) photographed c. 1910 with a tipi painted with elegant elk designs. See box on page 14 for more about tipis.**

Each of the three Blackfeet tribes held an annual Sun Dance in a specially constructed "Medicine Lodge." In spite of government pressures, the Sun Dance has been held through the present time. As late as 1958, the Bloods still held the Medicine Pipe Dance by the Horn Society, the strongest Native religious group surviving. Their main deities were the Sun and a supernatural being, Napi, or "Old Man." Their dead were placed in trees, or sometimes in tipis erected for the purpose, on hills.

During the nineteenth century, Blackfeet numbers declined from some 15,000 to about 6,750 in 1862: Many died of starvation when the buffalo finally disappeared. After 1877, the Canadian Blackfoot settled in three Alberta reserves: the North Blackfoot near Gleichen, the North Piegan near Brocket, and the Blood at Cardston. The South Piegan were finally restricted to a reservation on the eastern side of Glacier National Park, Montana, with the administrative agency at Browning. These Blackfeet had established relations with the U.S. fur companies on the Missouri and suffered terribly in smallpox outbreaks. In the years after 1884, following the collapse of their hunting economy, Blackfeet struggled to adjust to white rural life, farming, and stock-raising, and more recently to an industrial wage economy. The Montana (U.S.) division is officially called Blackfeet.

In contrast to pre-reservation days, Blackfeet culture is now often socially divided by religion, social achievement, and ancestry. In the recent past, however, a renewed awareness of Indian culture has led to increased participation, even by those of mixed ancestry, in Pan-Indian powwows, which are often performed several times a year. The South Piegans promote the annual North American Indian Days on their reservation at Browning, Montana, and similar events are held by the Bloods, North Piegans, and North Blackfoot; but the sacred bundles have mostly fallen into disuse. The Blackfeet historically made beautiful clothing—elaborately decorated warrior attire of shirts and leggings with eagle feather headdresses, and full-length buckskin women's dresses,

BLACKFEET BONNET

Also called the war bonnet or circle bonnet. This typically has a wide, beaded buckskin brow band. The Blackfeet almost always hang strings of seed or pony beads from the bottom edge of the rosettes. The base of each feather is bound with red, blue, or green cloth, felt, or wool. These bases are then wrapped with several bands of horizontal or diagonal thread or tape binding. This binding is sometimes referred to as "firecrackers" and is usually white or yellow. The tips of each feather have circles of fur, skin, paper sealing wax, or even chewing gum, that are 1 inch (2.5 centimeters) in diameter, as an added feature. Major plumes and crown feathers are usually missing; base "fluffies" can be of any color, although white is considered the best type. This golden eagle feather headdress was given to Sir Douglas Bader, the British World War II fighter pilot, in 1957 during his adoption as honorary chief of the Blood Band of the Blackfoot Indians of Alberta, Canada.

(See also box on page 41.)

Above: **Blackfeet parfleche, c. 1870. Parfleches were folded envelopes of rawhide— untanned buffalo or other skin —which can be molded when fresh and wet, and which dries hard, waterproof but semi- flexible. Usually folded from a single sheet, with flaps secured by thongs through burnt holes, they were used for carrying dried food and clothing. The Blackfeet made additional holes allowing attachment to saddle or travois frame. They were painted, usually only on the end flaps, with bold designs in pigments mixed with buffalo hoof glue. Characteristically smaller than most, Blackfeet parfleches tended to have curved designs and triangles in solid colors.**

adorned with rich beadwork. This ceremonial dress, although modified over the years, is still worn at modern powwows, together with an ever-changing array of dancers' attire. The Blackfeet population in 1970 was 18,000, of whom 9,900 were Montana Blackfeet, largely of mixed descent, and only half now resident on the Blackfeet Reservation. In 1970, the Bloods numbered 4,262, the North Piegan 1,413, and the North Blackfoot 2,355, all in Alberta, Canada. In 1996, the Bloods alone numbered over 8,000. Census 2000 reported 27,104 Blackfeet.

Right: **Inside a Blackfeet Medicine tipi, c. 1910. The pipe altar is center foreground. Behind it is the pipe bundle; the pipe bowl is attached to tripods in the background.**

The Cheyenne lived on the High Plains and were an important Algonkian tribe whose earliest known home was present-day Minnesota, between the Mississippi and Minnesota rivers. When first recorded in 1680, they were farmers living in permanent villages by the Illinois River, but they gave up domestic skills such as agriculture and pottery after being driven out onto the Plains to become nomadic bison hunters. Their social groups were split into male age-graded societies. They lived in tipis, painted in geometric patterns, and developed the ceremony of the Sun Dance.

They were constantly pressed farther and farther west onto the Plains, however, by the Sioux (who later became their great allies) until they finally settled around the upper branches of the Platte River. Their cultural hero Sweet Medicine recorded how they were joined by a related tribe—the Sutaio—an event that took place at Bear Battle in the Black Hills of western South Dakota.

Below: **A view of the interior of an Arapaho or Cheyenne tipi.**

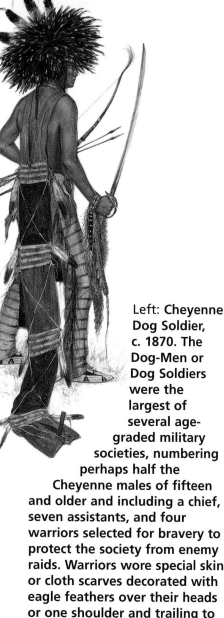

Left: **Cheyenne Dog Soldier, c. 1870. The Dog-Men or Dog Soldiers were the largest of several age-graded military societies, numbering perhaps half the Cheyenne males of fifteen and older and including a chief, seven assistants, and four warriors selected for bravery to protect the society from enemy raids. Warriors wore special skin or cloth scarves decorated with eagle feathers over their heads or one shoulder and trailing to the ground. Their supreme demonstration of bravery was to stake this to the earth with a red peg, symbolizing willingness to fight to the death on the spot.**

Right: **Cheyenne and Arapaho chiefs, 1859—the standing Indian figure is possibly Black Kettle (Southern Cheyenne)—photographed at Fort Leavenworth on their way to Washington, D.C. with interpreter John Smith. Photograph collected by William Blackmore, c. 1865**

The Cheyenne shared with the other Plains tribes features such as military societies (the Cheyenne had the Dog Soldiers), band divisions (of which the Cheyenne may have had up to ten), and the Sun Dance that they created. However, they differed in having a central council of forty-four chiefs and in their sacred tribal objects, the Medicine Arrows and the Sacred Buffalo Hat.

The tribe as a whole only came together in the summer when enough food was available for everyone. At least one great ceremonial was held then, the Sun Dance, the Animal Dance, or the Renewal of the Medicine Arrows. The Animal Dance, performed to ensure the supply of meat—particularly buffalo—featured the symbolic killing of animals by clowns or Contraries (a male society), who performed their rituals backward.

After establishing themselves on the upper branches of the Platte River in Wyoming and Colorado, the Cheyenne were in constant warfare with the Crow, Shoshone, and Pawnee. The tribe split geographically into the Northern and Southern Cheyenne, thanks to the building of Bent's Fort on the upper Arkansas River in Colorado (in 1832). This forced a large part of the tribe to move south to Arkansas, leaving the rest on the North Platte, Powder, and Yellowstone rivers.

By the early 1840s the Cheyenne had come across the white man and, before the cholera epidemic of 1849, numbered about 3,000. In 1851, the Fort Laramie Treaty recognized the two divisions of the tribe. Between 1854 and 1879, the Cheyenne fought more than fifty military actions against U.S. soldiers and consequently lost more fighting men in comparison with their numbers than any other Plains Indian people.

In 1864, Col. John M. Chivington led a troop militia against a camp of more than 500 unarmed Cheyenne and Arapaho at Sand Creek, Colorado, cruelly massacring many women and children. In 1866, Cheyenne warriors were with the Sioux who annihilated Capt. William J. Fetterman's troops near Fort Phil Kearny, Wyoming, but in September 1868 the Cheyenne military leader Roman Nose was killed at Beecher Island, on the Arikara River in eastern Colorado. In November of that year, Black Kettle's Southern Cheyenne village on the Washita River in Oklahoma was destroyed by Lt. Col. George A. Custer, and the following summer the Cheyenne Dog Soldiers under Tall Bull were defeated at Summit Springs, Colorado.

After the U.S. government failed to protect Indian hunting grounds from gold prospectors and railroad surveyors, as specified in the 1868 Fort Laramie Treaty, the Northern Cheyenne joined the Sioux as active participants against Custer's final campaign in Montana in 1876. The Sioux and Cheyenne forces surrounded and destroyed Custer and his troops at the Little Bighorn on June 25, 1876, but despite this victory, success was short-lived. Subsequently, Col. Ranald S. Mackenzie secured

CHEYENNE DRESSES

A Cheyenne woman's dress is made from three buckskin hides, with the two smaller hides used for fringes, extensions, etc. The front and back hides are trimmed into rectangles, then pieced together like a tube. The yoke or cape hide is folded and sewn on at 90 degrees to the body with the animal legs—or often false legs—hanging below the arms. Usually three bands of beadwork decorate the yoke. Typically two bands of beadwork are sewn halfway between the head end and the seam and one band along the shoulder fold. The hole for the head is a simple slit, laced up with thong. The dress is often decorated front and back with buckskin fringes with large beads, the fringe being simply laced in and out of the hide. Other beadwork, quillwork, fringes, and painting often decorate the dress. At the skirt bottom corners, extensions are attached to simulate the old animal legs.

Above: **Beautifully worked and beaded Cheyenne baby carrier.**

the Cheyennes' surrender and confinement to reservations. In 1877, a portion of the Northern Cheyenne were brought to Oklahoma to be colonized with the Southern Cheyenne, who had agreed to move to a reservation located in western Indian Territory under the terms of the Medicine Lodge Treaty of 1867.

Reservation conditions were harsh and became intolerable, causing Cheyenne chiefs Little Wolf and Dull Knife to lead their people in a heroic return to the north country in 1878. Despite being imprisoned at Fort Robinson, Nebraska, and making a second break for liberty, about 60 rejoined those who had remained in the north and in 1884 were assigned a reservation on the Tongue River, Montana, where their descendants remain. In this comparatively rugged, isolated country, Cheyenne descendants have struggled with problems of poverty and readjustment to rural, and recently urban, U.S. culture.

In 1954, the Northern Cheyenne numbered 2,120, but there has been an increase in the numbers of those of mixed Cheyenne and white ancestry in recent years; however, traditional beliefs surrounding the Sacred Buffalo Hat and the Sun Dance persist. The Southern Cheyenne are found in Custer, Roger Mills, Canadian, Kingfisher, Blaine, and Dewey Counties in Oklahoma, parts of the allotted Cheyenne and Arapaho Reservation opened to white settlement in 1892. In 1950, there were 2,110 Southern Cheyenne. They, too, have retained traditional symbols of ethnic unity, such as the Sacred Medicine Arrows. Although they are nominally Christian, the Peyote religion has a strong following in the south. In 1970, the Cheyenne numbered in total 6,872 and in 1990 totaled 10,829. Census 2000 saw the figure rise to 11,191.

CENSUS 2000

The numbers recorded for the Cheyenne were:

Cheyenne	5,310
Northern Cheyenne	5,555
Southern Cheyenne	323
Total	11,191

The Comanche spoke a Shoshonean language, and perhaps split from the Shoshone after obtaining horses during the late seventeenth century, to become the most skilled horsemen of the southern Plains and a truly nomadic people. They were then associated with the area around the North Platte River until driven south by the Sioux to land near the headwaters of the Cimarron, Brazos, Red, and Canadian Rivers. Fierce warriors as well as traders, they harried the Spaniards all the way into Mexico, replenishing their own herds of horses by trade or by attacks on settlements. They were at first enemies but later friends of the Kiowa, and together they often closed the Santa Fe Trail. They often adopted white women captured on their raids.

One of their first official dealings with Americans came in 1834, when Col. Henry Dodge met several Comanche representatives at a Wichita village on the Red River. They remained periodically hostile to Texans and U.S. citizens until the famous Medicine Lodge Council of 1867, held in Kansas just north of the Oklahoma state border and attended by thousands of southern Plains Indians. As a result of the Medicine Lodge Treaty and military action against the Cheyenne on the Washita River in 1868, the Comanche settled on a reservation in southwestern Indian Territory, now Oklahoma. Early reservation life was marked by much suffering, starvation, hostile outbreaks, and military reaction. The last of the Comanches to accept reservation life were the Kwahadi band under Quanah Parker, who surrendered in 1875. Parker, son of a white

Below: A **Comanche woman, wife of Milky Way, photographed by William Henry Jackson in 1872.**

Above: **Comanche warrior, c. 1840. The principal defense of the Plains warrior was the rawhide shield, usually made from the buffalo's thickest breast hide and protected, when not in use, with a soft buckskin case. Shields were painted with symbols and had small "medicine" attachments meant to confer power and protection on the warrior.**

captive, became an influential leader and the first recognized chief during early reservation life.

The Comanche had several subtribes, or bands, the best known being the Kwahadi or "Antelope" band, the Yamparika or "Yap eaters," the Nokoni, Tanima, Kutsveka, and Penateka or "Wasps," the most southern band and vanguard of the Comanche southward migration. Their bands were self-managing, with no large tribal government. For war, bands joined together and named a temporary chief. They decorated their buckskin clothing with heavy fringing rather than by beadwork or other decoration, and their tipis were built on a four-pole basis like those of their Shoshone relatives.

Their population has often been overstated; it was perhaps 4,000 in the early nineteenth century and 2,538 in 1869; reduced to 1,476 in 1910, it recovered to 4,250 in 1970, including a considerable amalgam of Spanish, Mexican-Indian, Anglo, and recently other Oklahoma Indian ancestry. The Comanche numbered 8,500 in 1993 and 10,120 in Census 2000, but only 250 elderly members were fluent in the language.

Most modern Comanches live in the rural and urban parts of Caddo, Kiowa, Comanche, and Cotton counties, in Oklahoma. The changes brought by adjustment to white American life have resulted in tribal disputes between liberals and conservatives, Christians and Peyotists, and "full-bloods" and "mixed-bloods."

Although the Comanche were renowned powwow dancers and singers, the Sun Dance was not an important aspect of their culture. The Comanche, together with the Kiowa, were principally responsible for the spread of the Peyote religion to other Oklahoma tribes. The Peyote religion, derived from Mexican Indians by way of Lipan and Mescalero Apaches, was adopted by the Comanche in the 1880s. Involving the sacramental eating of peyote, a mild hallucinogen, it mixes Native and Christian beliefs and developed in Oklahoma into its present two divergent rites. The Comanche have been actively involved with Oklahoma Pan-Indian powwows up to present times. They are a federally recognized tribe and elect their leaders.

Plains Cree is the term given to cover the Cree bands living partly or wholly on the prairies of Saskatchewan and Alberta, Canada, from the mid-eighteenth century. As a whole, the Cree Native group is Canada's largest, with 200,000 present day members registered. Culturally distinct from their Woodland Cree cousins, the Plains Cree adopted Assiniboine traits which are essentially "Plains" in format (notably, ceremonials and dependence on the buffalo) in common with the Blackfeet, Assiniboine, and Gros Ventre, whom the Plains Cree displaced from the Saskatchewan River. In the late eighteenth century, they were reinforced by bands of Swampy Cree who partially changed to the Plains culture but remained largely marginal. The marginal bands between the Swampy and Plains Cree were sometimes referred to as "Bush Cree." The total number of Plains Cree in the early nineteenth century may have been 15,000 before smallpox. Cree conquest of the western forest seems to have been complete by the late eighteenth century, and by about 1820 they were linked to the Assiniboine and venturing onto the Prairie. By 1876, most of the Plains Cree had submitted to Canadian authority, although they participated in the 1885 Métis uprising.

Plains Cree culture included using buffalo for meat and hides. The arrival of the horse, probably as early as 1750, helped their hunting and tribal movements. Their material culture also resembled the High Plains forms: the skin (later canvas) tipi, buckskin clothes, some tattooing, and ceremonial clothing with quillwork and beadwork in geometrical and later floralistic designs. Warrior and rank societies existed for men. The concept of a single all-powerful creator and supernatural power in all phenomena prevailed. They had the Sun Dance, also called Thirsting Dance, the vision quest, smoking tipi rite, medicine bundles, and other Plains ceremonies. The present Canadian population of specifically Plains Cree exceeds 20,000, with some 7,000 Plains Cree and Plains Ojibwa in Montana. The Cree language is spoken in five dialects by some 45,000 Crees in southern Canada and into Montana. The nine Plains Cree bands are:

Below: **The Plains Cree chief Poundmaker, photographed c. 1880 by G. Moodie, Maple Creek, Saskatchewan. This important Cree leader—an adopted son of the Blackfoot chief Crowfoot— was a guide for the Marquis of Lorne, governor general of Canada, during a visit to the West. He was later imprisoned for his part in the Northwest Rebellion in 1885 and died the following year. He gave his name to a band and reserve for his people (see River People page 29), which remains home to Plains Cree in Saskatchewan today.**

Above: **Plains Cree man, c. 1780.**
The Cree had penetrated the
northeastern Great Plains in
present-day Saskatchewan
and Manitoba by the late
eighteenth century. Surviving
evidence of male dress suggests
that these Plains people who
came originally from farther
east retained partly fitted hide
tunics and quilled and painted
decoration similar to the dress
of earlier Subarctic Algonkians.

CALLING RIVER
Of the Assiniboine and Qu'Appelle valleys, mostly
now under the File Hills and Crooked Lake agencies,
the Calling River or Qu'Appelle Cree were a
marginal division of the "Bush" Cree and have
mixed considerably with the Plains Ojibwa.

CREE–ASSINIBOINE
An extension of the Calling River band in association
with the Assiniboine and probably a mixture of the two
tribes, located near the Wood and Moose mountains
(Saskatchewan), now mostly under the File Hills-
Qu'Appelle Agency (Piapot's band) and Crooked Lake
Agency (White Bear). Mr. N. J. McLeod, Superintendent
of the File Hills-Qu'Appelle Agency, in a well-
documented description of the Cree and Saulteaux at
the agency, claims: "Piapot's Band are of the Plains
Cree tribe of Indians, and are somewhat different
from other Cree tribes, in that they are descendants
of Indians who lived by hunting the buffalo, whereas
some of the Cree tribes lived along the fringes of the
bush areas and are known as Willow or Bush Crees,"
establishing them as marginal, in sharp contrast to
Piapot's band.

TOUCHWOOD HILLS
Between Long Lake and Touchwood Hills, now largely
on the Poormans, Day Star, and Gordons reserves.

RABBITSKINS
Roaming the Assiniboine River between the Calling
River and Touchwood Hills bands, with whom they
are now mixed under the File Hills-Qu'Appelle and
Touchwood agencies, the Rabbitskins were a "Bush"
group connected to trading posts during the
nineteenth century, at which time they were
associated with Bungi or Plains Ojibwa.

HOUSE PEOPLE
Living near the junction of the North and South
Saskatchewan rivers, mostly above the north branch.
The House People were partly "Bush Cree" and partly
true Plains Cree. They now live principally on the

Mistawasis and Sandy Lake (Ahtahkakoops) reserves under the Shellbrook Agency.

PARKLANDS PEOPLE
A "Bush" or Willow Cree group on the South Saskatchewan near its junction with the north branch, they are now under the Duck Lake Agency at Beardy's and Fort-a-la-Corné reserves. These were a late extension of the Swampy Cree under fur trader influence.

RIVER PEOPLE
On and below the north branch of the Saskatchewan River and the Battle River, these are true Plains people and one of the largest Plains Cree groups. Their descendants are mostly on the Poundmaker, Sweet Grass, Red Pheasant, and Little Pine reserves of the Battleford Agency. They were closely related to the Alberta or Beaver Hills Cree.

BEAVER HILLS PEOPLE
The largest, most important division of the Prairie Cree, they inhabited Saskatchewan beyond Onion Lake, Neutral Hills, and Beaver Hills to the headwaters of the Saskatchawan River. They are now mostly at these reserves: Onion Lake (Saskatchewan), Saddle Lake, Alexander, Ermineskin, Samson, Montana, Sunchild, and John O'Chiese, under the Saddle Lake, Edmonton, Hobbema, and Stoney-Sarcee agencies. On many reserves they have mixed with their old allies, the Assiniboine, and former enemies, the Blackfeet and Sarsi.

ROCKY BOY AND UNITED STATES CREE
As the American fur trade on the Missouri grew during the early 1800s, Plains Cree, Swampy Cree, and Métis wandered in small groups through Montana and North Dakota. After the second Métis rebellion in Saskatchewan in 1885, some Plains Cree removed to Montana to escape the Canadian authorities. A reservation called Rocky Boy near Havre (Montana) was established for landless Plains Cree and Plains Ojibwa in 1916, but many more remained landless refugees on several reservations in Montana.

Above: **Plains Cree Indians photographed in Saskatchewan, c. 1890.**

CENSUS 2000 (U.S.)

The numbers recorded for the Cree were:

Cree	2,488
Rocky Boy's Chippewa Cree	5,531

Below: **A heavily decorated Plains Cree or Plains Ojibwa saddle.**

Right: **Crow dancers, c. 1885.**

Below Right: **Modern dancers at the annual Crow Fair, Montana, including those in traditional attire, a fancy dancer, a young girl shawl dancer, and, in the background, a dancer with a "jingle" dress. Originating among the Chippewas of Minnesota late in the nineteenth century, this dress is decorated with long tin cones that jingle.**

Below: **Two Crow men, c. 1910. The man on the right holds a horse memorial effigy, which would be used at a ceremonial dance to represent a deceased but honored or favorite horse.**

An important Siouan tribe of the northwestern Plains who, in the 1600s, split from the Hidatsas (an agricultural people living in earthen lodges on the Missouri River) to become nomadic buffalo hunters. In time, the Crow were divided into two main bands: the River Crows, who lived along the Missouri and Yellowstone rivers, and the Mountain Crows, in the mountain valleys of southern Montana and northern Wyoming. A third, smaller band called "Kicked in the Bellies" derived their name from their first interaction with the horse.

The Hidatsas themselves had once been three distinct groups: the nomadic Awaxawi, the older settled agriculturalists the Awatixa, and the Hidatsa proper, the last of the group to move to the Missouri River from the east, who learned to cultivate corn from the Mandans. The Mountain Crow probably separated from the Awatixa, and later the River Crow from the Hidatsa. A map, produced in 1805 under the direction of William Clark, located the "Paunch Indians" (Mountain Crow) and the "Raven Indians" (River Crow) separately. The last Crow separation from the Hidatsa was under way by the middle of the eighteenth century, although an association remained until an outbreak of smallpox in 1782 most probably hastened the split.

The disastrous second smallpox epidemic in 1837 cut trading ties, destroyed the Mandans, and partly destroyed the Hidatsas and Arikaras. These peoples, particularly the Mandans, had long been resident in the valley of the upper Missouri River in settled farming villages of earth lodges in what is now North Dakota. When the exploring Vérendrye brothers ventured onto the Plains west of the main Hidatsa and Mandan villages in 1738–39, they reported another Hidatsa-type people, who would probably be the later Mountain Crow but were then still apparently earth lodge dwellers. By the time of

Above: **Crow Chief Curley, his wife, and Chief Long Tail, c. 1907. Curley was a noted Army scout of the Custer campaign of 1876.**

TRIBAL RIGHTS AND BUSINESSES TODAY
Many tribes today have re-secured their land rights through skilled litigation. A number have reclaimed their tribal status in order to take advantage of non-tax and other dispensations previously accorded to them through treaty. These often include gaming rights, allowing a number of tribes to invest in gaming operations that enrich their communities. Profits often go toward building hospitals, schools, and cultural centers and creating jobs that improve the standard of living for both Indians and the areas in which they live.

Lewis and Clark's epic journey of 1804–06, they lived along the middle course of the Yellowstone River (River Crow) and the mountainous regions of the upper course (Mountain Crow), one of the richest territories of the Great Plains for natural resources.

The Crows had continued links with their Hidatsa kinsmen for a hundred years through trade. The ideally positioned Mandan and Hidatsa villages on the Missouri River became a center of an indigenous trade system that drew a succession of white traders following in the footsteps of the Vérendryes. The relative abundance of material culture and population stability—before the ravages of smallpox—led to elaborate social and religious structures, clan systems, annual religious ceremonialism, and a rich and varied artistic background which remained with the Crows long after it was extinguished among the Missouri River peoples. Their clan system was unique among High Plains nomads, reflecting their Hidatsa origin.

Through their connection with the Hidatsas, the Crows were also able to obtain surplus agricultural products and ultimately white trade goods in exchange for horses, hides, skins, and dried meat. In turn, the Crows traded with the Nez Perces to the west and the Shoshones to the south, from whom they obtained huge numbers of horses. Trade included guns, knives, and Indian corn in exchange for buffalo robes and leather clothing and promoted sharing of tribal art styles. Such intertribal trade continued via the Plateau tribes to the peoples of the Columbia River. This secondary trading route ultimately was a main source of transmitted craft and art styles in which the Mountain Crows and the "Kicked in the Bellies" clan group shared ceremonial dress such as men's buckskin shirts, parfleches, and horse gear with their Plateau friends. Crow cradles and incised rawhide decoration certainly show Plateau influence, while religious organizations such as the Tobacco Society and social societies continued to reflect their Hidatsa connections.

Prior to the Lewis and Clark expedition of 1804–1806, few white men had seen the Absarokee or Crow Indians, although the Vérendryes had visited them in 1743 and called them *Beaux Hommes* (beautiful men). After Lewis and Clark came various fur traders, and trading posts such as Forts Liza and Cass forged permanent white contacts with the Crows. The artist George Catlin portrayed them as one of the most colorful Native tribes on the northern Plains in the 1830s.

By 1864, the Bozeman Trail led right through Crow country, and it was followed by the building of military forts (Reno, Phil Kearny, and C. F. Smith) to protect white immigrants. On the whole, Crow relations with whites, though often strained, remained largely peaceful. They signed treaties with the United States in 1825 and recognized their boundaries as defined by the Fort Laramie Treaty of 1851. A second Laramie Treaty in 1868 established the Crow Reservation, although this was subsequently reduced in area. The present Crow Reservation is south of Billings, Montana, in Bighorn County. The administrative center is the Crow Agency.

The Crows have fared better than most Indians in their adaptation to U.S. culture, although they are still distinctively Indian and hold the colorful Crow Indian Fair each August. In 1869, the last traditional Crow chief, Chief Plenty Coups, insisted that the federal government provide education for his people, which helped them maintain their language and culture. The Montana tribe's mineral rights provide significant funding for schools, including a community college. They originally numbered perhaps 8,000 before smallpox reduced them. In 1944 there were 2,467; in 1954, 3,416; in 1970, 3,779; and in 1991, 8,491. Census 2000 gives 9,117—a figure rising to 13,394 when all respondents are included.

Above: **Burial scaffold, probably Crow, Montana, c. 1900. The scaffold provided a means of exposing the body to the elements for a natural return to the environment.**

Below: **Shavings, a Crow chief photographed in Montana in 1880. He wears a typically resplendent Crow shirt, panel leggings, and moccasins with animal tails hanging from the heels—probably signifying warrior status.**

Right: **A Kiowa beaded cradle, c. 1890.**

Below: **The Kiowa warrior Tape-Day-Ah ("Standing Sweat House"), c. 1875; he was reputed to have been a member of every Kiowa war party between 1870 and 1874. Note the southern style of tailored, fringed shirt, decorated fur turban, and bow case and quiver made from mountain lion skin.**

According to their own tradition, the Kiowas' earliest known home was in Montana, and they were in possession of the Black Hills of western South Dakota during the eighteenth century. They were probably expelled from this region by the Sioux arriving from the east and began a movement south to the Arkansas and the headwaters of the Cimarron River and northern Texas. By 1790, they had established friendly relations with the Comanche. At some time, perhaps in the late seventeenth or early eighteenth centuries, a small Athabascan tribe, the Kiowa Apache, joined them and remained as a subtribe until reservation days. The Kiowa developed into a formidable and typical Plains tribe. Their language forms an independent family but is distantly related to the Tanoan family of Pueblo Indians. Despite ravaging the southern Plains and even northern Mexico with their Comanche allies, they developed a lucrative trade relationship with the Pueblos.

They became known to the Americans in the early nineteenth century and were reported on the prairies of the Arkansas and Red Rivers in 1820. A treaty at Fort Atkinson in 1853 attempted to establish peace on the Santa Fe Trail, which ran through Kiowa territory, but with little success. The Kiowa suffered from the cholera epidemic of 1849 and from smallpox in 1861. Despite their reduced numbers and agreements (1865 and 1867) to exchange their tribal lands for a reservation in southwestern Indian Territory, now Oklahoma, they continued to raid Texas. These raids climaxed in the fight at Adobe Wells in 1874, after which the Kiowa chief Satanta was arrested and later committed suicide. Some Kiowa warriors were even imprisoned and sent for three years to Florida. Much of Kiowa history was contained in a pictographic form known as "calendar histories," recorded by the ethnologist James Mooney.

By the late 1870s, the Kiowa and Comanche were finally restricted to their reservation in southwestern Oklahoma, suffering further tragedies from epidemics and starvation after the disappearance of the buffalo in 1879. Their transition from tribal to reservation life was attended by much misery. Their population before the epidemics of the early nineteenth century may have been more than 2,000 but was barely a thousand by the time of their final surrender at Fort Sill in 1875. In 1924, they were reported to number 1,699, and in 1970 numbered 4,357, with a considerable percentage of Mexican and other Indian ancestry, particularly Comanche.

The present population of Kiowa live mainly in Caddo County, Oklahoma, with the largest community near Carnegie. After several decades of dormancy, a Kiowa warrior society has been revitalized, lending a distinctively Kiowa flavor to Oklahoma Pan-Indianism in the form of the "Gourd Dance." This society has now been formally organized in four separate factional divisions that promote Kiowa ethnic identity among both rural and urban tribal members. Gourd Dance members are often invited to attend powwows throughout Oklahoma; they sing and dance holding distinctive rattles and fans. In 1992, there were almost 10,000 enrolled Kiowas, but their language was spoken by less than 400 people. By the 2000 census, the figures had changed to a total of 12,242 Kiowa and part Kiowa, of whom some 339 were enrolled in Oklahoma.

Below: **Kiowa warrior, c. 1875. The Kiowa of the southern Plains, often allied with the Comanche, were known for painted and fringed hide garments. Some shirts and leggings were painted yellow or blue-green with twisted fringing, but at this period they used only minimal edge and seam beadwork. Here his otter fur turban with trailer is decorated with ribboned and beaded rosettes. This man has an otter skin bow case and quiver, with strike-a-light and whetstone cases hanging from the latter; he carries a painted rawhide shield. In later years, the use of lances seems to have been largely ritualistic, as firearms became more widely available.**

Below: **Mandan Buffalo Bull Dancer, c. 1833, after the work of artist Karl Bodmer. A member of the Buffalo Bull Society, who imitated the motions and sounds of the animal when dancing, he wears a bison's head mask, carries a shield, and holds a lance, perhaps of a ceremonial type similar to the bow-lances and society staffs of other tribes.**

The largest and most important of the three upper Missouri River horticultural tribes, who lived in dome-shaped earth-covered lodges stockaded into villages. They planted maize, beans, and pumpkins, but also hunted bison. The Mandans no doubt once resided somewhere near the Mississippi Valley and the heartland of agricultural North America. The Winnebagos were perhaps their closest relatives, but their speech shows a long separation from their parent Siouan family, and they entered their historic North Dakota region several generations before the Hidatsas. Prior to the 1782 smallpox epidemic, they outnumbered the three Hidatsa villages, with perhaps 3,800 people.

Their first recorded contact with whites was in 1738, when Pierre Vérendrye visited them, at which time they had nine villages near the Heart River in modern North Dakota. By the time Lewis and Clark wintered alongside them in 1804 these had been reduced to only two, Metutehanke and Puptari, below the mouth of the Knife River on the west bank of the Missouri River. During the 1830s, artists Karl Bodmer and George Catlin painted some of the best scenes of Native America ever recorded, including Mandan chiefs, villages, and important, complex religious ceremonies such as the Okeepa, similar to the Sun Dance.

In 1837, smallpox largely destroyed the Mandan: only 137 people reportedly survived. They joined the Hidatsas and were settled on the North Dakota Fort Berthold Reservation, where a few descendants perpetuate their name. In 1906 they numbered 264, and in 1937 totaled 345, but they are now largely merged with the Hidatsa.

Left: **Meraparpa or Lance-Mandan, probably photographed during a Mandan and Arikara delegation to Washington, D.C., in 1874. His buckskin shirt is decorated with quillwork strips; his hair is wrapped in fur, and the three upright, decorated eagle feathers perhaps signify his warrior status.**

Below: **Straight-up eagle feather headdress which belonged to Mato Toope (Four Bears), a Mandan. Collected by Prince Maximilian von Wied in 1833.**

Together with the Arikara they form the "Three Affiliated Tribes of North Dakota (Fort Berthold)." Among the ceremonies observed by the three tribes, the Okeepa warrants special attention because of its complexity and great antiquity. It is a four-day spectacle involving self-torture, the drama of "Lone Man" who saved the tribe from disaster, and other origin myths.

The Mandan villages in their prime were a key trade center for nomadic Plains tribes and the northern tribes: Both agricultural products and material culture spread from them over a wide area. Village reconstructions can be seen at Mandan at Knife River near Stanton, North Dakota, and Fort Abraham Lincoln State Park, North Dakota.

CENSUS 2000

The numbers recorded for the Mandan were:	
Mandan	369
Three Affiliated Tribes of North Dakota (Fort Bethold)	3,508

Tribal names are—for the most part—not the old names the Indians knew themselves. Many names translate simply as the "real men" or "original people." The common, popular, modern names used are derived from various sources. Some are from Native terms, either from the people themselves or names applied by neighbors or enemies, or corruptions of these terms. Some tribal names are anglicized (made English) forms of translated Native names; others are from French or Spanish sources. We use the tribal names most commonly encounte red in history and literature, although it should be noted that some modern Indian groups have successfully reintroduced their own names into current usage.

Below: **Pawnee Tribal Council, Oklahoma, 1939. For this photograph they are wearing attire from their own and other tribes.**

The largest and most important tribe of the Caddoan linguistic family, the Pawnee were probably the last to migrate in a northeasterly direction, reaching the valley of the Platte River in Nebraska. They were essentially an agricultural people, cultivating corn, beans, squash, and pumpkins; they also hunted buffalo and other game that was abundant in Pawnee territory in early times. While in Nebraska, they lived in four groups of earth lodge villages, each with its own chief, council, and medicine bundles: the Skidi or Wolf Pawnee, Pitahauerat or Tapage Pawnee, Kitkehahki or Republican Pawnee, and the Chaui or Grand Pawnee. Through their sacred bundles, shrines, priests, and religious ceremonials, they felt connected with supernatural cosmic forces that could heal diseases, call forth game, and ensure plentiful harvests. They believed that all these were created by one deity — Tirawa.

The Pawnees' first contact with Europeans was probably with the Coronado expedition in 1541; a guide in his party is thought to have been a Pawnee. They obtained horses from the Spanish settlements, however, beginning in the seventeenth century, Pawnees were often captured by the Apache, who sold them as slaves to the Spanish and Pueblo Indians in

New Mexico. French traders, allied with them by 1750, provided them with guns to fend off the Apache. Contact with immigrants through Pawnee territory brought decimation from cholera and smallpox, reducing their population from perhaps 10,000 in 1838 to about 1,300 in 1880. In a succession of treaties with the U.S. government, they ceded all their lands except for a reservation in present Nance County, Nebraska; but in 1874–76 all four bands moved to Indian Territory (now Oklahoma), where an agency and reservation were established below the Arkansas River adjoining the Osage. However, their so-called "surplus" lands—after the infamous allotments were completed—were opened to white settlement in 1893. Pawnee rural descendants still live in and around Pawnee and Skedee, Pawnee County, Oklahoma. They numbered about 1,260 in 1950, 1,928 in 1970, and 2,500 in 1990, with many having a large proportion of white and non-Pawnee Indian ancestry.

They still sponsor the Pawnee Homecoming Powwow each summer, to which other tribes are invited and to which Pawnee men serving with the U.S. Army often return, a military tradition that goes back to the nineteenth century. The Pawnee, never at war with the United States, often served as scouts for the U.S. Army against their common enemy, the Sioux. Their powwow is of the popular pan-Indian type established in Oklahoma during the early twentieth century, derived from the cultural blending of many tribes forced to move to Oklahoma during the second half of the nineteenth century. The songs and dances are based on old Ponca, Kaw, and Osage forms, in turn influenced by Omaha, Sauk, and Fox warrior society rituals. Spreading far beyond the tribes who developed it, the Oklahoma powwow is now a highly successful continuation of Indian ceremonialism.

Above: **An earth lodge, probably Pawnee—as suggested by the extended vestibule. Better insulated and more permanent than tipis, each lodge housed several families during planting and harvesting seasons. Twice annually, in June and October, the Pawnee left their villages to live in tipis that were often large enough to shelter up to eighteen people during their summer and winter buffalo hunts. The Pawnee revered their staple corn, calling it "mother." They used all parts of the buffalo—including the stomach, which they made into cooking and water vessels. They also hunted raccoons, quail, skunks, prairie chickens, and otters.**

CENSUS 2000

The numbers recorded for the Pawnee were:

Oklahoma Pawnee	32
Pawnee	2,453
Total	2,485

SIOUAN

An important language family whose original speakers probably originated in the Mississippi Valley, where some of the most highly developed North American civilizations flourished. Tribal traditions seem to indicate movement from this general area northwestward along the Missouri, ultimately dominating the central Plains. However, a divergent branch, the Catawba and their associates are found in the Carolinas; and late-nineteenth-century texts collected on the Iroquois Grand River Reserve in Ontario from adopted Tutelo descendants strongly suggest a close relationship to the western division of the family. The Western Siouans are the Dakota-Assiniboine group, comprising the Dakota, Nakota, and Lakota (including the seven great Sioux tribes in three linguistic sections) and the Assiniboine; the Dhegiha, comprising the Omaha, Ponca, Kansa, Osage, and Quapaw; the Chiwere, comprising the Iowa and the Oto-Missouri; the Winnebago, Mandan, and finally the Hidatsa-Crow.

*S*ioux is a collective term used by the United States and Canadian governments to designate the largest section of the Siouan linguistic family—seven tribes, all very closely related. When first mentioned by the early white explorers in the mid-seventeenth century, all seven tribes lived within what is now the southern half of the state of Minnesota. Several of the tribes have a tradition of residence at Mille Lacs, Minnesota, which seems still to have been a home for several bands when the French explorers Louis Hennepin and Daniel Duluth visited them in 1678.

Culturally they seem to have originally been a Woodland and Prairie people, living in bark lodges and practicing slash-and-burn horticulture, fishing, and hunting. The name *Sioux* seems to be of Ojibwa-French extraction, meaning "adders." Pressure during the eighteenth century from the Ojibwa, who were supplied with firearms by the French, pushed the Sioux westward. Several tribes crossed the Missouri River and developed a strong horse culture and were dependent upon the bison, tipi dwelling, and a nomadic way of life. In time they became known for their intense resistance to white encroachment.

Their own name, Dakota, means "allies." *Dakota* is the name of the whole nation in the eastern dialect, *Nakota* in the middle dialect, and *Lakota* in the western dialect. The seven tribes were: the Mdewakanton, the

THE WAR BONNET

A symbol of the American Indian: the eagle feather crown or war bonnet. Feather crowns are probably ancient in the Americas, associated with chieftainship, war, and ritual. The flared crown bonnet probably evolved among the upper Missouri River tribes and was recorded in this form by the painter George Catlin as early as the 1830s. It was particularly associated with the Sioux, Cheyenne, and Arapaho, but during early reservation days was adopted by many tribes as an ethnic symbol. The feathers were laced to a hide skullcap (or, later, a traded felt hat with the brim removed). (See box on page 19.)

Wahpekute, the Wahpeton, and the Sisseton, forming the Dakota or Santee section; the Yankton and Yanktonai, forming the Nakota or middle section; and the Teton, forming the Lakota or western branch. In 1990, 75,000 Sioux descendants were reported in the United States, perhaps 20 percent of full ancestry. They are discussed below in alphabetical order.

MDEWAKANTON SIOUX A Sioux tribe of the Eastern or Santee division who formerly lived at Mille Lacs at the head of the Rum River but later in the region of the west bank of the Mississippi River from Winona to Red Wing in southeastern Minnesota. The economy of the Santee relied on hunting, fishing, gathering (especially wild rice), and horticulture. They lived in bark gable-roofed houses and wigwams. Bison hunts were organized by appointed hunt chiefs, and band chiefs were usually hereditary, with *akicita* (police) appointed from the warrior societies. Dress was modified during the eighteenth and early nineteenth centuries by the adoption of cloth, sashes, and coats from traders; but they retained shirts,

Left: **Red Shirt or Bear Stop, a Minneconjou Teton Sioux, had been a warrior at the time of the Custer battle of June 1876 and later was with Sitting Bull at the Yellowstone River when he held talks with Col. Nelson A. Miles. While Sitting Bull moved north to Grandmother's Country (Canada), Red Shirt returned to the Standing Rock Agency. Later a "Red Shirt" toured with Buffalo Bill's Wild West shows and was photographed here at Earls Court, London, c. 1910, when he was reported as an Oglala Sioux.**

CENSUS 2000

The numbers recorded for the Sioux were:

Blackfoot Sioux	412
Brule Sioux	73
Cheyenne River Sioux	9,064
Crow Creek Sioux	2,550
Dakota Sioux	1,739
Flandreau Santee Sioux	336
Fort Peck Sioux	2,233
Lake Traverse Sioux	21
Lower Brule Sioux	1,687
Lower Sioux Indian Community of Minnesota Midwakanton Sioux	418
Midwakanton Sioux	436
Miniconjou	35
Oglala Sioux	22,157

Continued on page 45

leggings, and soft-soled moccasins. Santee women wore the two-piece Central Algonkian-style dress consisting of a wraparound skirt and loose blouse. The Santee were expert at ribbonwork and beadwork, including floral, animal, and geometrical designs applied to ceremonial dress. Their chief ceremonies were the Medicine Dance, which resembled the Algonkian Midewiwin, and Thunder Dance; some bands also adopted the Sun Dance.

In 1851, they sold their lands to the U.S. government and moved to the upper Minnesota River area. They were the principal participants in the uprising against the whites in Minnesota, the disastrous Dakota War of 1862, which resulted in their capture and dispersion. Some fled to Canada under their chief Little Crow, while others were placed principally on the Santee Reservation, Knox County, Nebraska (mixed with Wahpekute); Upper Sioux Reservation near Granite Falls; Lower Sioux Reservation near Morton; Prairie Island near Red Wing; Prior Lake near Shakopee (all in Minnesota); and the Flandreau settlement on the Big Sioux River, South Dakota. Before 1851, there were seven bands of Mdewakanton. The Santee of the Niobrara Reservation, Nebraska, numbered 1,075 in 1904 and 1,400 in 1955, but many had left the area. A few are in Canada at Sioux Valley (Oak River) and Birdtail near Birtle, Manitoba, but not separately reported.

SISSETON SIOUX The largest of the four Eastern Sioux or Dakota tribes, who claim an origin around the headwaters of the Rum River, Minnesota, near Mille Lacs. Later they seem to have been located about the junction of the Minnesota and Blue Earth Rivers and at Traverse des Sioux. By the 1840s, some had moved to Lake Traverse and the James River

Below: **Sioux Indians gambling, c. 1909, probably at a Wild West touring show; several men are wearing beaded vests (waistcoats) and blanket strips, hairpipes, and feather bonnets.**

GAMBLING GAME PRACTISED BY THE AMERICAN INDIANS.

country. The majority were located on the Sisseton Reservation in South Dakota and combined with the Wahpeton. A few joined other Santee at Oak River (Sioux Valley), Manitoba, and more of their descendants are at Standing Buffalo Reserve near Fort Qu'Appelle and Moose Woods or White Cap Reserve near Dundurn, both in Saskatchewan. In 1956, the Sisseton-Wahpeton at Lake Traverse (Sisseton Reservation) numbered 3,672; in 1970, Standing Buffalo numbered 514, and Moose Woods, 148. Before they were forced out of Minnesota following the Dakota War of 1862, there were about six bands including those of Sleepy Eyes, Red Iron, and Gray Thunder, all prominent chiefs. The band called "Dryers on the Shoulder" lived near Lake Traverse and were great buffalo hunters; they apparently formed the principal group of the Standing Buffalo Reserve in Canada.

TETON SIOUX The largest and most powerful of all the original seven branches of the Sioux, in fact outnumbering the other six tribes together. They became the Western Sioux or, in their own dialect, Lakota, following their migration onto the High Plains in the late eighteenth and early nineteenth centuries. They were divided into seven bands: Hunkpapa, Minneconjou, Sihasapa (or Blackfoot—no connection with the Algonkian Blackfeet), Oohenonpa (Two Kettle), Sicangu (or Brulé), Itazipco (Sans Arcs), and Oglala. Leaving their original home in Minnesota, they lived around Lake Traverse by 1700 and on the Missouri by 1750; by about 1820 they claimed the whole of western South Dakota surrounding the Black Hills. They changed completely to a bison-hunting economy supplemented by deer and antelope, lived in conical skin tipis, and secured vast herds of horses.

The Western Sioux had an elaborate system of warrior societies, including the *akicita* or police, Kit Foxes, Crow Owners (referring to a special type of

Above: **Geometric lazy stitch beadwork on a Sioux man's waistcoat.**

Below: **The so-called "Red Cloud shirt," as worn by Red Cloud and other Teton Sioux (Lakota) chiefs in the late nineteenth century. This magnificent garment is now in the Buffalo Bill Historical Center, Cody, Wyoming.**

Left: **Western Sioux tobacco bag, c. 1890.**

Below : **Eastern Sioux brave, c. 1860s, probably photographed in Minnesota by J. E. Whitney. Note his gunstock-shaped wooden club and his pipe with its twisted stem and catlinite bowl, typical of western Woodland groups.**

dance bustle), and Strong Hearts (famous for their unique ermine-skin, horned headdresses worn in battle). These societies fought as a unit whenever possible. Warfare and hunting were important male activities. Another type of organization, completely mystical in character, became the dream societies such as Buffalo and Elk Dreamers. Although details of organization differed from band to band, the council and chiefs emerged as the principal governing body. The supreme councilors among the Oglala were "Shirt-Wearers." Their dress consisted of skin shirts and leggings for men decorated with porcupine quills or later beads; women wore skin dresses, often heavily beaded; much decoration was in characteristic geometric designs. The Sun Dance was the great focal point of summer camps. They also had Yuwipi, a night society, probably Woodland in origin, and the "shaking tipi rite." Burial was invariably on scaffolds; "winter counts" were pictographic calendar histories on buffalo robes.

The California Gold Rush of 1849 and the discoveries of gold in Colorado and Montana in the 1860s brought white men in greater numbers across Western Sioux lands, killing buffalo. The Sioux became resentful, attacking wagon trains and prospectors and outfighting soldiers. Finally, at the treaty of Fort Laramie in 1868, Chief Red Cloud demanded that white men be kept out of their country—that the Great Sioux Reservation, the whole of present South Dakota west of the Missouri—be reserved exclusively for Sioux use. For a few years the treaty held, until, in 1874, gold was discovered in the Black Hills, traditionally a sacred area. This, together with the U.S. government's complete inability to keep white prospectors, immigrants, and hunters out of the area, led to a series of bitter conflicts which climaxed in the destruction of General Custer's troops in June 1876 on the Little Bighorn River, Montana, and the ultimate surrender of Crazy Horse in 1877 and Chief Sitting Bull in 1881. The Great Sioux Reservation was divided into smaller reservations—Pine Ridge, Rosebud, Lower Brulé, Cheyenne River, and

Standing Rock—followed by further losses of land and the subsequent sale of unoccupied areas (allotments).

This began, for the Sioux, many years of impoverished reservation life, with poor housing, few job opportunities, restrictions on religious ceremonies, and the boarding school system, which took children away from their families in an attempt to strip them of their own culture. Today, there is a wide racial and cultural range on the Sioux reservations and, in large part because of this history, many remain troubled by social problems.

The distribution of the modern Western or Lakota Sioux is as follows: the Hunkpapa are mostly at Standing Rock Reservation and a few at Wood Mountain Reserve, Saskatchewan; the Minneconjou are at Cheyenne River Reservation; the Sans Arc, Sihasapa, and Two Kettle are also at Cheyenne River; the Upper Brulé are at Rosebud Reservation; the Lower Brulé at the Lower Brulé Reservation; and the Oglala at Pine Ridge Reservation, although there has been some mixing. It was at Pine Ridge that the Wounded Knee massacre of Indian people took place in 1890, during the Ghost Dance movement; this has become a tragic symbol of Indian subjection by whites and was the last important military engagement between whites and Indians.

Despite poor surroundings, the Sioux have a tremendous spirit, and many retain traditional pride and openness of character. Much of the belated understanding and reverence for Indian culture today stems from the activities of modern Sioux people. During the 1860s, the Grass Dance (named for sweetgrass braids worn by the participants) or Omaha Dance was adopted by the warrior societies as their own rites fell into disuse. The lively songs and male dances became a main social activity at Indian gatherings on reservations and quickly spread to most northern Plains tribes. For years only men participated, but in recent times

Above: **Wahpeton and Yanktonai Sioux dancers, c. 1900, probably at a Fourth of July Powwow, Fort Totten Reservation, Devils Lake, North Dakota.**

Continued from page 42

Pine Ridge Sioux	771
Pipestone Sioux	1
Prairie Island Sioux	219
Shakopee Mdewakanton Sioux Community (Prior Lake)	95
Rosebud Sioux	14,037
Sans Arc Sioux	1
Santee Sioux of Nebraska	1,987
Sioux	21,886
Sisseton-Wahpeton	5,115
Sisseton Sioux	672
Spirit Lake Sioux	2,430
Standing Rock Sioux	8,714
Teton Sioux	5,326
Two Kettle Sioux	1
Upper Sioux	84
Wahpeton Sioux	64
Yankton Sioux	4,941
Yanktonai Sioux	2
Total	108,272

women and children have taken part as well. Today, as in the past, powwows are held on all reservations.

In 1904, the Lakota were distributed as follows: Cheyenne River, 2,477; Lower Brulé, 470; Pine Ridge, 6,690; and Rosebud, 4,977—when added to the Middle and Eastern branches they totaled 26,175, including Assiniboine, within the United States. In 1956, there were 4,983 enrolled at Cheyenne River; 705 at Lower Brulé; 9,875 at Pine Ridge; and 8,189 at Rosebud. In 1970, there were 47,825 Sioux (Western, Middle and Eastern) in the United States and 5,155 in Canada (the only Teton representatives in Canada are 70 people at Wood Mountain). Today a large number of Sioux live in Denver. There were approximately 57,000 Western Sioux descendants alone in 1993.

WAHPEKUTE SIOUX A branch of the Santee or Dakota division on the Cannon and Blue Earth Rivers in southern Minnesota. Lewis and Clark found them on the Minnesota River below the Redwood River junction. After the sale of their lands in 1851, some joined the Mdewakanton. Following their participation in fighting in Iowa and Minnesota in the 1850s and 1860s, the Wahpekute fled mostly to Canada and west to the Missouri. Those on the Missouri combined with the Mdewakanton on the Santee Reservation on the Niobrara River, Knox County, Nebraska, where about 400 of their descendants remained in 1955.

In Canada, where some descendants of Chief Inkpaduta's band remain, they live on Sioux Valley Reserve (Oak River) near Griswold, Manitoba, mixed with the three other Santee tribes, numbering 899 in 1970. A few others were incorporated among other Santee at Oak Lake near Pipestone, Manitoba, and

Below: **Delegation of Brulé Sioux (Lakota) to Washington, D.C., June 1870. Left to right: Fast Bear (Mato Ohanco), a senior warrior of the Wazhazha band; Spotted Tail (Sinte Galeska), head chief of the Brulé subtribe; Swift Bear (Mato Luza), chief of the Corn Owners band; Yellow Hair, another senior warrior of the Wazhazha. Right rear is Capt. D. C. Poole, to whose Carlisle Indian School in Pennsylvania children were often forcibly sent for insensitive indoctrination in white ways.**

Sioux Wahpeton Reserve (Round Plain) near Prince Albert in Saskatchewan. In the United States, a handful probably merged with the few Mdewakanton in the small remaining Minnesota communities, and a few more are said to have accompanied the Yanktonai to Fort Peck, Montana.

Most of the Eastern Sioux have over the years assumed the rural culture of the European immigrant farmer, but at a generally lower economic level. The Wahpekute today do not exist as a separate tribal group, having mixed with other communities after the 1862–63 Minnesota campaign during which Gen. Henry H. Sibley and his troops scattered the Santees, many fleeing to Canada.

WAHPETON SIOUX The traditional home of the Wahpetons was around Little Rapids, some 45 miles (72 kilometers) from the mouth of the Minnesota River's junction with the Mississippi, but after 1851 they removed to Lac-Qui-Parle and Big Stone Lake in western Minnesota. They were involved in the war between the Eastern Sioux and Minnesota whites in 1862, as a result of which they were scattered over a wide area. Ultimately, most were gathered on the Sisseton or Lake Traverse Reservation in South Dakota where, in 1909, the combined Sisseton-Wahpeton numbered 1,936. A few Wahpeton were included with Sisseton and Yanktonai at Devil's Lake (Fort Totten) Agency, North Dakota, where the three together numbered 1,013 in 1904. In 1956, the population at Sisseton was 3,672, and at Devil's Lake (Fort Totten), 1,500. A number also fled to Canada, their descendants in Manitoba at the Birdtail Reserve near Birtle numbering 187 in 1970, and those at Long Plain Sioux Reserve near Portage La Prairie, 224. These are mostly Wahpeton

Above: **A Teton (Western) Sioux woman and child, c. 1885, probably at Rosebud or Pine Ridge Reservation, South Dakota. Both wear Plains Indian metalwork on belts, decorated moccasins, and dresses made from trade cloth.**

Below: **A Sioux storage or tipi bag.**

descendants, as are a few mixed with other Santee at Oak River, Oak Lake, Manitoba, and Standing Buffalo and Round Plain, Saskatchewan. The Eastern Sioux in Minnesota and Yankton have traditionally been the only persons who possessed the rights and permissions to work the pipestone quarries of southern Minnesota, where ceremonial pipes and, more recently, souvenirs were made.

YANKTON SIOUX One of two divisions forming the Nakota or Middle Sioux. They probably lived in the vicinity of Mille Lacs with their relatives during the seventeenth century. In 1708, they were on the east bank of the Missouri River near the site of Sioux City, Iowa; they were not separately noted again until Lewis and Clark encountered them along the James, Big Sioux, and Des Moines Rivers in southeastern South Dakota; in 1842 they were noted on the Vermillion River in South Dakota. They seem to have been well known to traders along the Missouri, and through the efforts of Chief Palaneapape they were restrained from joining the Santee in the Minnesota fighting of 1862.

In 1858, they ceded all their lands to the United States, except for a reservation on the north bank of the Missouri near Wagner, South Dakota, where their descendants have lived ever since. They were generally indistinguishable from their close relatives the Yanktonai. Lewis and Clark estimated their numbers at 4,300 with the Yanktonai. In 1867 there were 2,530 Yanktons alone; in 1909 they were reported as numbering 1,739; in 1945, 1,927; and in 1956, 2,391. A few incorporated with other Sioux on various reservations and are no longer reported separately, and many have married with non-Indians over the years; perhaps fewer than half of the present inhabitants of

Above: **Western Sioux headdress.**

reservations in eastern South Dakota are full-blood members of their respective tribes. The Yankton are said to have had eight bands, the Cankute or "Shooters-at-the-Tree" being the most noted.

YANKTONAI SIOUX The more dominant of the two Nakota branches of the Sioux nation, speaking the same dialect as the Yankton. Their homeland included the drainages of the James and Big Sioux Rivers and the Coteau du Missouri. The economy of these Middle Sioux, like the Missouri River groups they had displaced, rested on a base of hunting, fishing, gathering, and river bottom horticulture. Great tribal bison hunts took place twice a year, taking them far west of the Missouri. They used the skin tipi and skin-covered wickiups resembling those of bark found among the Santee; they also made or used abandoned earth lodges. They employed the "bull boat," a round hide river craft probably adopted from the Mandan, Hidatsa, and Arikara. The Sun Dance was their most important religious ceremony. The Yanktonai divided into two divisions: the Upper Yanktonai in six bands, and the Lower Yanktonai or Hunkpatina. (In the seventeenth century, the Assiniboine are said to have divided from the Yanktonais and moved to Canada.)

The Yanktonais took part in the War of 1812 on the side of Great Britain. They took no part in the Dakota War of 1862, and made treaties of peace with the United States in 1865, being divided between reservations on the Missouri. The Upper Yanktonai descendants are on the Standing Rock Reservation on the North–South Dakota border and on the Devils Lake (Fort Totten) Reservation, North Dakota. The Lower Yanktonais are found on Crow Creek Reservation, Fort Thompson, South Dakota, and on the Fort Peck Reservation, Wolf Point, Montana. In 1956, the combined Sisseton-Wahpeton-Upper Yanktonai of Fort Totten numbered 1,500; the combined Tetons and Upper Yanktonais of Standing Rock 4,324; the Lower Yanktonais and Tetons of Crow Creek 1,132; and the Lower Yanktonais (locally called Yanktons) and Assiniboines of Fort Peck were reported as 3,881.(See page 45 for 2000 Census information.)

Above: **Eastern Sioux warrior, Wa-kan-o-zhan-zhan (Medicine Bottle), who was executed in November 1865 for his part in the Minnesota uprising, or Dakota War of 1862. Photographed by J. E. Whitney in June 1864 at Fort Snelling, Minnesota. Near starvation on their reservation along the upper Minnesota River, the Dakota Sioux rebelled against broken treaties and dishonest agents by attacking the Redwood and Yellow Medicine Indian Agencies and all whites living on their former lands, killing more than 450 whites. The Sioux lost the war and thirty-eight warriors were executed in the largest mass execution in U.S. history.**

CENSUS 2000

The numbers recorded for the Assiniboine Sioux were:

Assiniboine Sioux	1,384
Fort Peck Assiniboine and Sioux	356
Total	1,740

ARIKARA or REE
The third of the upper Missouri River horticultural tribes, a Caddoan people and a relatively late offshoot of the Skidi Pawnee. In the 1780s, French traders reported them below the Cheyenne River in modern South Dakota. In 1804 Lewis and Clark encountered them between the Grand and Cannonball Rivers close to the present boundary between North and South Dakota, and found them already weakened in numbers due to smallpox. The Arikara were also often on unfriendly terms with the Mandan, Hidatsa, and surrounding Sioux. In 1862, they finally joined the Hidatsa and Mandan on the Fort Berthold Reservation, North Dakota, where their descendants have since remained. Despite their early hostility to Americans, some Arikara served as scouts for the U.S. Army. Census 2000 records their numbers as 775.

GROS VENTRE or ATSINA
An Algonkian tribe of the northern Plains, considered once part of the Arapaho but for much of the nineteenth century they were allies of the more powerful Blackfeet. Their French name ("big belly") apparently derives from the movement of the hands over the abdomen to indicate hunger in the Plains Indian sign language used by Indians of differing speech to communicate. Their home for most of the nineteenth century was between the South Saskatchewan River in Canada and the Missouri River in Montana, particularly around the Milk River. Census 2000 records 2,881 Gros Ventres, including 1,300 Fort Belknap Gros Ventres.

HIDATSA or MINITAREE
A Siouan tribe of the upper Missouri River in North Dakota who, according to tradition, came from somewhere to the northeast but met and allied themselves with the Mandan and shared with them the agricultural pursuits for

which they have become renowned. They were in reality a group of three closely related village tribes—Hidatsa, Awatixa, and Awaxawi. Before this time, but after their arrival on the Missouri, the people later called Crow had split from the Hidatsa after a dispute. The Hidatsa movement to the Missouri has been put as early as c. 1550. In 1837, a terrible smallpox epidemic reduced them to a few hundred survivors consolidated in one village, which was moved in 1845 to Fort Berthold, where they have resided ever since. Census 2000 reports 624 Hidatsa, a figure that swells to 1,335 when all respondents with part Hidatsa heritage are included.

IOWA

A small Siouan tribe who lived on the Blue Earth River, Minnesota. Later they were located near the Platte River in Nebraska, Iowa, and northern Missouri. In 1824, they agreed to move from their homeland, along with some of the Sauks and Foxes, to Great Nemaha Reservation in northeastern Kansas, where they settled in 1836. During the allotment (breaking up for sale to whites) of the Nemaha Reservation, a number of Iowas moved to seek homes in Indian Territory and, in response to a plea to government officials, were assigned a reservation in present Payne and Lincoln counties, Oklahoma, to the west of the Sauk and Fox of Oklahoma. The Iowas spoke a dialect of the Chiwere branch of the Siouan family, being closely related to the Oto and Missouri and more distantly to the Winnebago. (See box at right for Census 2000 figures.)

KANSAS, KANSA or KAW

An important Siouan tribe of the Dhegiha group, very closely related to the Osage. They lived on the Republican, Kansas, and Big Blue Rivers in northern Kansas and adjacent Nebraska. Their western advance was checked by the Cheyenne. In 1815, the Kansa were said to have 130 earth lodges and a population of 1,500. A government agent estimated them at 1,850 in 1822, but they were drastically reduced by smallpox over the next few years. They first agreed with the U.S.

Left: **Birohka or Hidatsa, painted by Karl Bodmer in 1833. He is wearing a magnificent painted buffalo robe and turban.**

CENSUS 2000

The numbers recorded for the Iowa were:

Iowa	1,000
Iowa of Kansas and Nebraska	333
Iowa of Oklahoma	118
Total	1,451

Below: **A Plains bag.**

Below: **Omaha man, c. 1868.**
His clothing is characteristic of
the Missouri Valley tribes. The
otter fur turban is decorated
with ribbonwork and beaded
at the front with the hand
motif common among the
Omaha, Osage, and Pawnee.
Grizzly bear claw necklaces
were characteristic of the
southern Woodlands and
Prairies, although never
numerous because of the
difficulty of obtaining them
(particularly from the now-
extinct Plains grizzly).
Highly valued, the claws
were considered to be
imbued with the strength
and valor of the bear.

authorities to move to a reservation at Council Grove on
the Neosho River in 1846, where the Kaw Indian Mission
still stands. These lands were directly on the Santa Fe
Trail, however, and in a succession of agreements they
were finally persuaded to move to Indian Territory (now
Oklahoma) in 1873. Census 2000 records 1,150 Kaws.

KICHAI or KITSAI
A Caddoan tribe who were living on the upper Trinity
River in Texas in 1701, probably midway between the
tribes that became collectively either Caddo or Wichita.
Some were part of the Indians who moved to the Wichita
Agency, Indian Territory, from the Brazos Reservation in
Texas in 1859. In 1977, with no speakers of Kichai out
of a population of 350, their language was considered
extinct. Their descendants are counted as Wichita today
and live in rural Caddo County, Oklahoma.

MISSOURI
A small Chiwere Siouan tribe, at one time the same
people as the Oto, with a tradition of a past separation
from the Winnebago. Later the Missouri and Oto divided,
the former living for a time on the Grand River, a branch
of the Missouri in present northern Missouri, while the
Oto moved to the Des Moines River in Iowa. Wasted by
wars with the Sauk, Fox, Osage, and Kansa as far back
as 1748, they reunited several times with the Oto.
Finally about 90 Missouris joined the Oto on the Big
Blue River and accompanied them to Oklahoma, where
the two tribes became officially the Otoe-Missouri Tribe
of Oklahoma. (See page 53 for U.S.Census figures.)

OMAHA
A Siouan tribe of the Dhegiha dialectic group who are
thought to have moved west from the Mississippi Valley,
perhaps even from the Ohio Valley. Some as yet
unverified evidence may link these Siouans with the
Mound Builders, the ancient people who built the great
earthworks of southern Ohio. The Omaha continued
along the Missouri for about 800 miles (1,290 km) above
its confluence with the Mississippi. In 1820, the Omaha
had a permanent village in present Dakota County,
Nebraska; they planted corn, beans, pumpkins, and

watermelons and were also employed in obtaining furs for white traders. In 1854, they ceded their lands to the United States in return for a reservation in Thurston County, Nebraska, a portion of which was ceded to the Winnebago in 1865. (See U.S. Census figures, lower right.)

OSAGE

The largest and most important Dhegiha Siouan tribe, part of a Siouan movement which divided into the Omaha, Ponca, and Kansas, who ascended the Missouri River—the Quapaws going south to the Arkansas while the Osages remained on the Osage River in central-western Missouri. Their hunting territory extended to the west, which brought them into contact (and continuous enmity) with the High Plains Kiowas and Comanches. Although Osage tribal life and religion existed until the late nineteenth century, they had a long association with various Spanish and French traders with whom they sometimes joined in marriage, which gave them a reputation for haughty "Latin" manners.

The Osage made several treaties with the United States during the early nineteenth century, by which they ceded their lands in Missouri and Oklahoma for part of southeast Kansas centering in present Neosho County. After the opening of these lands to white settlers following the Civil War, they faced intolerable conditions; however, the sale of remaining lands allowed the purchase of a reservation in Indian Territory, now Osage County, Oklahoma. Having recovered from the many difficulties they suffered in Kansas, the Osage found themselves in possession of oil and mineral deposits on their reservation during the late 1890s and early 1900s, which brought great wealth to some Osage families.

Above: **An Osage man wearing a fur turban and ball and cone metal earrings, c. 1890.**

CENSUS 2000	
Omaha	4,239
Osage	7,658
Otoe-Missouria	1,470

OTO or OTOE

A Siouan tribe of the Chiwere group with a history of a separation from the Winnebagos and a later separation from the Missouri Indians near the mouth of the Iowa River. They gradually moved west, first to the Des Moines River, then to the Missouri River, then to an area on the south side of the Platte River in southeastern Nebraska. Never prominent in history, the Oto were always a small group who lived among enemy tribes. They are now in Oklahoma.

PADOUCA

Early in the eighteenth century the Padoucas are recorded as a people of western Kansas and usually considered as Comanche. However, several historians have suggested that they may have been Apachean—perhaps even the first great tribe to have attempted to form settlements and grow crops in the heart of the High Plains country (although archaeological evidence now suggests that the early agriculturalists, at least, were Puebloan). If they were indeed Apachean, perhaps the Lipans and Kiowa Apaches were all that were left of them by the nineteenth century. Recently the Comanche theory seems more acceptable to historians. A tribe reported as Gatakas seem to have been close allies of the Kiowas, and this was probably an early term for the Kiowa Apaches, or alternatively part of a composite "Padoucas" who moved south through the Great Plains before the Kiowas and Comanches but who subsequently disappeared from history, at least under that name.

PLAINS OJIBWA or BUNGI

Groups of Woodland Ojibwas first established themselves on the edges of the Plains by about 1790, and later some bands became true High Plains Indians. They left their homelands in Minnesota and Ontario and finally occupied an area of southwestern Manitoba, northern North Dakota, and southeastern Saskatchewan. The great expansion of the Ojibwas began in the eighteenth century after they secured firearms from the French and English. Those who lived on the northern edges of the Prairies are often called Saulteaux (pronounced "sotoe"), but those who successfully adapted their culture to life on the Plains are Plains Ojibwa or Bungi, although no sharp division actually existed.

PONCA

A branch of the Omaha Indians who separated from their parent tribe. Ponca villages were usually located on a river or creek terrace where they could cultivate gardens on nearby bottom lands. They were usually at war with the Sioux. By treaty in 1858, they ceded their lands to the United States for a reservation at the mouth of the Niobrara River, which the Poncas were forced to leave in 1876–77 for Indian Territory, where they were finally given lands on the Salt Fork of the Arkansas River. (See U.S. Census box at right.)

QUAPAW or ARKANSEA

A member of the Dhegiha Siouan group, they were the most southern of the group. According to tribal traditions, they continued down the Mississippi into present Arkansas, while others turned up the Missouri River. By 1761, they had merged with ruined tribes, notably the Illini, while the Quapaw remained the nucleus of a diminishing people. In 1818, the Quapaw

Above: **A Plains Ojibwa family (probably Manitoba), c. 1880. Outside their tipi, a woman holds her child in a cradleboard of a Woodland form which has a double curved head bow guard. The tipi (canvas), a Plains type of dwelling, indicates the intermediate position the Plains Ojibwa held between Woodland and Plains cultures.**

Above left: **Medicine Horse, of the Oto tribe, wearing a fur turban and holding a metal trade tomahawk. A Zeno Shindler photograph, 1872.**

Below Left: **Oto buckskin leggings, decorated with graceful Prairie style floral beadwork, c. 1880.**

CENSUS 2000

The numbers recorded for the Ponca were:

Nebraska Ponca	190
Oklahoma Ponca	153
Ponca	3,012
Total	3,355

ceded all their lands to the United States except for a strip between Little Rock and Arkansas Post below Gillett, Arkansas. This was ceded in 1835 for lands in southern Kansas and northern Indian Territory, which in turn were ceded except for a section in the northeastern corner of Indian Territory, now Ottawa County, Oklahoma. This became the Quapaw Reservation but was allotted in 1895, with a subsequent loss of some of their land. Census 2000 recorded 1,151 Quapaw and 1,032 part.

SARSI or SARCEE (TSUU TINA)
A small Athabascan-speaking tribe who once lived along the upper Saskatchewan River in present Alberta, Canada. They joined the Blackfeet for protection against their enemies, the Crees and Assiniboines, perhaps some time in the late eighteenth century. Their customs thereafter were greatly modified by their long residence among the Blackfeet. They seem always to have been a small tribe and were decimated by smallpox in 1836 and scarlet fever in 1856.

SHUMAN or JUMANO
A people who from early Spanish reports were associated with various places in Texas and adjacent states, once thought to have been Caddoan, Apache, or Uto-Aztecan. They were reported on the Rio Grande in 1535 and were trading in eastern Texas in 1685. They are not clearly reported after 1740; if they were indeed Caddoan, then some may have merged with the Wichita; more probably, the last of them joined the Spanish-influenced groups around El Paso, Texas, and in Mexico, where a descendant was still living at Senecú in 1897.

TAWAKONI

A tribe of Caddoan speech and of the Wichita group who lived on the Arkansas River in present Muskogee County, Oklahoma, but who subsequently drifted south into Texas after the close of the French and Indian War in 1763. They were with the Wacos on the Brazos River near present Waco, Texas, in 1779 and were among the tribes on the Brazos in 1859 when persuaded to move, along with the Caddos, to a reserve on the Washita River in Indian Territory. They ultimately affiliated with the Wichita people and are no longer reported separately.

WACO

These Caddoan people were in northern Texas by 1779 under this name. Part of the people moved in 1859 from the Brazos River to the Washita River, Indian Territory, where they combined with the Wichita and are no longer reported separately.

WICHITA

The largest known historic tribe of the southern Caddoan-speaking group, who lived along the Canadian River in present-day Oklahoma. Government relations began in 1834 when Colonel Dodge from Fort Gibson, Indian Territory, held a council with the Wichita and other tribes on the North Fork of the Red River. They were hard hit by smallpox in 1837 and in 1859 they agreed to settle on a reservation south of the Canadian River, where they were joined by most of their relatives and by the Caddo with their associates from the Brazos Reserve in Texas. They were disrupted by the U.S. Civil War and, impoverished, were subsequently allotted lands by 1901. Census 2000 recorded 1,936 Wichitas including Keechies, Wacos, and Tawakonies as well as those who are part Wichita.

Left: **A series of photographs showing the deconstruction of a tipi. While they are not all of the same structure, the sequence does show the process well.**

Top: **"Wolf Tipi," Sarsi, Alberta, c. 1900. The designs were "transferred" to new canvas tipi covers as the old ones wore out. There are still painted lodges among the Blackfoot and Sarsi today.**

Center: **Sarsi Indians removing a canvas tipi cover from the pole frame.**

Below: **Sarsi Indians removing tipi poles, Alberta, c. 1900.**

Below: **Wichita grass house of Southern Caddoan tribal type, Anadarko, Oklahoma. The Wichita called themselves Kitikiti'sh, or racoon eyes.**

GLOSSARY

Agency. Represents the federal government on one or more Indian reservations under the Bureau of Indian Affairs (BIA), which is headed by a presidentially appointed commissioner. Many agencies, especially in the nineteenth century, were corrupt and often took financial advantage of the Indians they were supposed to manage and support.

Allotment. Legal process, c. 1880s–1930s, by which land on reservations not allocated to Indian families was made available to whites.

Anthropomorphic. Having the shape or characteristics of humans; usually refers to an animal or god.

Appliqué. Decorative technique involving sewing quills (usually porcupine) and seed beads onto hide or cloth, using two threads, to create a flat mosaic surface.

Apron. Male apparel, front and back, which replaced the breechcloth for festive clothing during the nineteenth and twentieth centuries.

Bandolier bag. A prestige bag, with a shoulder strap, usually heavily beaded, worn by men and sometimes women at tribal dances, common among the Ojibwas and other Woodland groups.

Birch bark. Strong, thick bark used for canoes and various wigwam coverings as well as for a wide variety of containers that were adapted for the European souvenir trade by the addition of colored porcupine quills, such as those produced by the Mi'kmaq and by the Ojibwas and Odawa of the Great Lakes area.

Buckskin. Hide leather from animals of the deer family—deer (white-tailed deer in the East, mule deer in the West), moose, or elk—used for clothing. The hides of buffalo, bighorn sheep, Dall sheep, mountain goat, and caribou were less commonly used.

Bureau of Indian Affairs (BIA). Begun in 1824, transferred from the War Department to the Department of the Interior in 1849. Now, around half of the BIA's employees are Native American, and the Bureau provides services through its agencies in many big cities as well as on rural reservations.

Coiling. A method of making pottery in the American Southwest, in which walls of a vessel are built up by adding successive ropelike coils of clay.

Confederacy. A group of peoples or villages bound together politically or for defense (e.g., Iroquois, Creek).

Cradles. Any of three main devices used across the continent to transport or carry babies: the cradle board of the Woodland tribes (cloth or skin attached to a wooden board with a protecting angled bow), the baby-carrier of the Plains (a bag on a frame or triangular hood with a cloth base folded around the baby), and the flat elliptical board covered with skin or cloth, with a shallow bag or hide straps, of the Plateau.

Drum or Dream Dance. A variation of the Plains Grass Dance adopted by the Santee Sioux, Chippewa (Ojibway or Ojibwa), and Menominee during the nineteenth century. Among these groups the movement had religious features that advocated friendship, even with whites.

Ethnographer. An anthropologist who studies and describes individual cultures.

Hairpipes. Tubular bone beads made by whites and traded to the Indians, often made up into vertical and horizontal rows called breastplates.

Lazy stitch. A Plains technique of sewing beads to hide or cloth, giving a final ridged or arch effect in lanes about eight or ten beads wide.

Leggings. Male or female, covering ankle and leg to the knee or thigh (male), usually buckskin or cloth.

Longhouse. The religion of conservative Iroquois, whose rituals still take place in special buildings also called longhouses.

Medicine bundle. A group of objects, sometimes animal, bird, or mineral, contained in a wrapping of buckskin or cloth, that gave access to considerable spiritual power when opened with the appropriate ritual. Mostly found among the eastern and Plains groups.

Moiety. A ceremonial division of a village, tribe, or nation.

Pan-Indian. A description of the modern mixed intertribal dances, costumes, powwows, and socializing leading to the reinforcement of ethnic and nationalist ties.

Parfleche. A rawhide envelope or box made to contain clothes or meat, often decorated with painted geometrical designs.

Peyote. A stimulant and hallucinogenic substance obtained from the peyote buttons of the mescal cactus.

Peyote Religion. The Native American Church, a part-Native and part-Christian religion originating in Mexico but developed among the Southern Plains tribes in Oklahoma, which has spread to many Native communities.

Powwow. Modern celebration, often intertribal and secular, held on most reservations throughout the year.

Prehistoric. In American Indian archaeology, a Eurocentric view of Indian life and its remains dated before A.D. 1492.

Rawhide. Usually hard, dehaired hide or skin used for parfleche cases, moccasin soles, shields, and drum-heads.

Reservation. Government-created lands to which Indian peoples were assigned, removed, or restricted during the nineteenth and twentieth centuries. In Canada they are called reserves.

Roach. A headdress of deer and porcupine hair, very popular for male war-dance attire, which originated among the eastern tribes and later spread among the Plains Indians along with the popular Omaha or Grass Dance, the forerunner of the modern War and Straight dances.

Sinew. The tendon fiber from animals, used as thread for sewing purposes.

Sweat lodge. A low, temporary, oval-shaped structure covered with skins or blankets, in which one sits in steam produced by splashing water on heated stones as a method of ritual purification.

Syllabics. A form of European-inspired writing consisting of syllabic characters used by the Cherokee in the nineteenth century and in other forms by the Cree and Inuit.

Termination. Withdrawal of U.S. government recognition of the protected status of, and services due to, an Indian reservation.

Tipi bag. Bags, usually buckskin, used for storage inside tipis.

Tobacco or pipe bag. Cases for men to carry ceremonial tobacco and pipes, usually made of buckskin that is beaded or quilled with fringing, made by most Plains peoples .

Tribe. A group of bands linked together genetically, politically, geographically, by religion, by a common origin myth, or, most often, by a common language. The term "Tribe" often arouses controversy: Many prefer "Nation" or "People." Ethnographers often use the word to describe people in fragmented or small groups who themselves recognize no such association.

War dance. Popular name for the secular male dances developed in Oklahoma and other places after the spread of the Grass Dances from the eastern Plains-Prairie tribes, among whom it was connected with war societies. . Many tribes had complex war and victory celebrations.

MUSEUMS

The United States naturally has the largest number of museums, with vast holdings of Indian material and art objects. The Peabody Museum of Archaeology and Ethnology at Harvard University, in Cambridge, Massachusetts, has over 500,000 ethnographic objects pertaining to North America, including a large number of Northwest Coast pieces. Many collections of Indian artifacts in major U.S. institutions were assembled by ethnologists and archaeologists who were working for, or contracted to, various major museums, such as Frank Speck and Frances Densmore for the Smithsonian Institution, Washington, D.C., or George Dorsey for the Field Museum of Natural History, Chicago.

Since the sixteenth century, the material culture of the Native peoples of North America has been collected and dispersed around the world. These objects, where they survived, often found their way into European museums, some founded in the eighteenth century. Unfortunately, these objects usually have missing or incomplete documentation, and because such material was collected during the European (British, French, Spanish, Russian) and later American exploration, exploitation, and colonization of North America, these collections may or may not accurately represent Native cultures. Collectors in the early days were usually sailors (Captain Cook), soldiers (Sir John Caldwell), Hudson's Bay Company agents, missionaries, traders, or explorers.

During the twentieth century, a number of museums have developed around the collections of private individuals. The most important was that of George Heye, whose museum was founded in 1916 (opened 1922) and located in New York City. It was called the Museum of the American Indian, Heye Foundation. This collection has now been incorporated into the National Museum of the American Indian, a huge building sited on the Mall in Washington, D.C., scheduled to open in September 2004. Other notable privately owned collections subsequently purchased or presented to scholarly institutions are the Haffenreffer Museum Collection at Brown University, Rhode Island; much of Milford G. Chandler's collection, which is now at the Detroit Institute of Arts; Adolph Spohr's collection at the Buffalo Bill Historical Center, Cody, Wyoming; and the impressive Arthur Speyer collection at the National Museums of Canada, Ottawa.

Many U.S. and Canadian museums and institutions have been active in publishing popular and scholarly ethnographic reports, including the Glenbow-Alberta Institute, the Royal Ontario Museum, Toronto, and, pre-eminently, the Smithsonian Institution, Washington, D.C. Most of the major U.S. museums have organized significant exhibitions of Indian art, and their accompanying catalogs and publications, often with Native input, contain important and valuable information.

In the recent past, a number of Indian-owned and -run museums have come into prominence, such as the Seneca-Iroquois National Museum, Salamanca, New York; the Turtle Museum at Niagara Falls; Woodland Cultural Centre, Brantford, Ontario, Canada; and the Pequot Museum, initiated with funding from the Pequots' successful gaming operation in Connecticut. The Pequots have also sponsored a number of Indian art exhibitions. Many smaller tribal museums are now found on a number of reservations across the United States.

There has also been much comment, debate, and honest disagreement between academics (Indian and non-Indian alike), museum personnel, and historians about the role of museums and the validity of ownership of Indian cultural material in what have been, in the past, non-Native institutions. Certain Indian groups have, through the legal process, won back from museums a number of funerary and religious objects, where these have been shown to be of major importance to living tribes or nations. The Native American Graves and Repatriation Act of 1990, now a federal law, has guided institutions to return artifacts to Native petitioners; some, such as the Field Museum of Chicago, while not strictly bound by this law, have voluntarily returned some remains and continue to negotiate loans and exhanges with various Native American groups. A listing of U.S. museums with Native American resources may be found at http://www.hanksville.org/NAresources/indices/NAmuseums.html.

FURTHER READING

Birchfield, D. L.(General Ed.): *The Encyclopedia of North American Indians*, Marshall Cavendish, 1997.

Brody, H.: *Maps and Dreams*, Jill Norman and Hobhouse Ltd, 1981.

Bruchac, Joseph: *Journal of Jesse Smoke: A Cherokee Boy: Trail of Tears, 1838*. Scholastic, Inc., 2001.

Buller, Laura: *Native Americans: An Inside Look at the Tribes and Traditions*, DK Publishing, Inc., 2001.

Coe, R. T.: *Sacred Circles: Two Thousand Years of North American Indian Art*, Arts Council of GB, 1976.

Cooper, Michael J.: *Indian School: Teaching the White Man's Way*, Houghton MIfflin Company, 1999.

Davis, M. B. (Ed.): *Native America in the Twentieth Century*, Garland Publishing, Inc., 1994.

Dennis, Y. W., Hischfelder, A. B., and Hirschfelder, Y: *Children of Native America Today*, Charlesbridge Publishing, Inc., 2003.

Despard, Yvone: *Folk Art Projects - North America*, Evan-Moor Educational Publishers, 1999.

Downs, D.: *Art of the Florida Seminole and Miccosukee Indians*, University Press of Florida, 1995.

Duncan, K. C.: *Northern Athapaskan Art: A Beadwork Tradition*, Un. Washington Press, 1984.

Ewers, J. C.: *Blackfeet Crafts*, "Indian Handicraft" series; Educational Division, U.S. Bureau of Indian Affairs, Haskell Institute, 1944.

Fenton, W. N.: *The False Faces of the Iroquois*, Un. Oklahoma Press, 1987.

Fleming, P. R., and Luskey, J.: *The North American Indians in Early Photographs*, Dorset Press, 1988.

Frazier, P.: *The Mohicans of Stockbridge*, Un. Nebraska Press, Lincoln, 1992.

Gidmark, D.: *Birchbark Canoe, Living Among the Algonquin*, Firefly Books, 1997.

Hail, B. A., and Duncan, K. C.: *Out of the North: The Subarctic Collection of the Haffenreffer Museum of Anthropology*, Brown University, 1989.

Harrison, J. D.: *Métis: People Between Two Worlds*, The Glentsaw-Alberta Institute in association with Douglas and McIntyre, 1985.

Hodge, F. (Ed.): *Handbook of American Indians North of Mexico*, two vols., BAEB 30; Smithsonian Institution, 1907–10.

Howard, J. H.: *Reprints in Anthropology Vol. 20:The Dakota or Sioux Indians*, J and L Reprint Co., 1980.

———: *Shawnee: The Ceremonialism of a Native American Tribe and its Cultural Background*, Ohio University Press, 1981.

Huck, B.: *Explaining the Fur Trade Routes of North America*, Heartland Press, 2000.

Johnson, M. J.: *Tribes of the Iroquois Confederacy*, "Men at Arms" series No. 395; Osprey Publishing, Ltd, 2003.

King, J. C. H.: *Thunderbird and Lightning: Indian Life in Northeastern North America 1600–1900*, British Museum Publications Ltd., 1982.

Lake-Thom, Bobby: *Spirits of the Earth: A Guide to Native American Symbols, Stories and Ceremonies*, Plume, 1997.

Lyford, C. A.: *The Crafts of the Ojibwa*, "Indian Handicrafts" series, U.S. BIA 1943.

Page, Jack: *In the Hands of the Great Spirit: The 20,000 Year History of American Indians*, The Free Press, 2003.

Paredes, J. A. (Ed.): *Indians of the Southwestern U.S. in the late 20th Century*, Un. Alabama Press, 1992.

Press, Petra, and Sita, Lisa: *Indians of the Northwest: Traditions, History, Legends and Life*, Gareth Stevens, 2000.

Rinaldi, Anne, *My Heart Is on the Ground: The Diary ol Nannie Little Rose, a Sioux Girl, Carlisle Indian School, Pennsylvania, 1880* (Dear American Series), Scholastic Inc., 1999.

Scriver, B.: *The Blackfeet: Artists of the Northern Plains*, The Lowell Press Inc., 1990.

Sita, Lisa: *Indians of the Northeast: Traditions, History, Legends and Life*, Gareth Stevens, 2000.

———: *Indians of the Great Plains: Traditions, History, Legends and Life*, Gareth Stevens, 2000.

———: *Indians of the Southwest: Traditions, History, Legends and Life*, Gareth Stevens, 2000.

Swanton, John R.: *Indian Tribes of the Lower Mississippi Valley and Adjacent Coast of the Gulf of Mexico*; BAEB 43; Smithsonian Institution, 1911.

Early History of the Creek Indians and Their Neighbors; BAEB 73; Smithsonian Institution, 1922.

———: *Indians of the Southeastern United States*; BAEB 137; Smithsonian Institution, 1946.

———: *The Indian Tribes of North America*; BAEB 145; Smithsonian Institution, 1952.

Waldman, Carl: *Atlas of The North American Indian*, Checkmark Books, 2000.

Wright, Muriel H.: *A Guide to the Indian Tribes of Oklahoma*, Un. Oklahoma Press, 1951..

This index cites references to all six volumes of the Native Tribes of North America set, using the following abbreviations for each of the books: GB = Great Basin and Plateau, NE = Northeast, NW = North and Northwest Coast, PP = Plains and Prairie, SE = Southeast, SW = California and the Southwest.

Lumbee: 25, 54 (NE); 33, 53, 56 (SE)
Lummi: 11, 43–44, 45, 47 (NW)
Lushootseed: 47 (NW)
Lutuamian (Lutuami): 53 (GB)

Mackenzie Inuit: 31 (NW)
Mahican: 12, 13, 14, 15, 24, 26, 50, 52 (NE)
Maidu: 35 (GB); 7, 11, 22–23 (SW)
Makah: 11, 38–39 (NW)
Malecite: 11, 25, 27, 48, 54 (NE)
Maliseet: see Malecite
Manahoac: 11, 51 (SE)
Mandan: 8, 9, 11, 30, 32, 36–37, 40, 49, 50 (PP)
Maricopa: 11, 26, 27, 46, 47 (SW)
Mascouten: 11 (NE)
Massachuset: (Massachusett) 11, 51 (NE)
Mattaponi 57 (NE)
Matinecock: 12, 53 (NE)
Mattole: 11, 13 (NW)
Mdewakanton Sioux: 11, 45 (PP)
Meherrin: 23 (NE); 56 (SE)
Menominee (Menomini): 23, 53 (NE)
Mescalero Apache: 11, 13, 15, 16, 17–18 (SW)
Mesquakie: see Fox
Methow: 11, 53 (GB)
Métis: 27 (PP); 19 (NW)
Me-wuk: see Miwok
Miami: 11, 49, 51, 52 (NE)
Micmac: 52, (NW); 11, 25, 27, 28–29, 38, 48 (NE)
Mikasuki: 44, 45 (SE)
Miluk: 53 (NW)
Minitaree: see Hidatsa
Missisquoi: 50 (NE)
Missouri: 9, 11, 41, 51, 52, 53 (PP)
Miwok: 7, 11, 24–25 (SW)
Mobile: 11, 51–52 (SE)
Moctobi: 47 (SE)
Modoc: 11, 35, 52, 53, 54 (GB)

Mohave: 11, 46, 47–48 (SW)
Mohawk: 11, 19, 23, 24, 25, 30–31, 38, 56 (NE)
Mohegan: 11, 26, 48, 50, 52, 54, 56 (NE)
Mohican: see Mahican
Mojave: see Mohave
Molala: 11, 50, 54 (GB)
Monacan: 11, 52 (SE)
Monache: see Western Mono
Moneton: 11, 52 (SE)
Mono: 11, 24–25, 33, 35 (GB)
Montagnais-Naskapi: 26, 54–55 (NW); 48 (NE)
Montauk: 11, 48, 50, 53 (NE)
Muckleshoot: 11, 43, 44, 47 (NW)
Mugulasha: 47 (SE)
Multnomah: 11, 23 (NW)
Munsee: 12,14, 26, 35 (NE)
Muskogean: 7, 12, 24, 26, 28, 34, 39, 40, 42, 46, 48, 50, 51, 53, 54, 55, 56, 57 (SE)
Muskogee (Creek): 8, 35, 36, 49 (NE); 8, 10, 12, 17, 18, 28, 29, 32, 34–39, 41, 42, 43, 45, 46, 47, 49, 50, 57 (SE)

Na-Dene: 28, 48 (NW)
Nahyssan: 11, 52 (SE)
Nambe Pueblo: 39 (SW)
Nanaimo and Snonowas: 44 (NW)
Naniaba: 52 (SE)
Nansemond: 56 (SE)
Nanticoke: 11, 13, 15, 48, 50, 53, 57 (NE)
Napochi: 11, 46 (SE)
Narraganset: 11, 48, 50, 53, 56, 57 (NE)
Natchez: see Taensa
Natchitoches: 11, 46, 51, 52 (SE)
Nauset: 57 (NE)
Navajo: 12 (NW); 32, 45 (GB); 9, 11, 12, 17, 30–32, 34, 44 (SW); 32 (NE)
Nespelem: see Sanpoil
Nestucca: 47 (NW)

Netsilik Inuit: 31 (NW)
Netsilingmiut: 31 (NW)
Neutral: 11, 24 (NE)
Nez Perce: 21 (NW); 8, 10, 11, 26–30, 38, 51, 54, 57 (GB); 32 (PP); 15 (NE)
Niantic: 11, 53, 54 (NE)
Nicola: 11, 12, 18–19 (NW); 56 (GB)
Nipmuc (Nipmuck): 48, 54, 55, 56 (NE)
Nisenan: 22, 23 (SW)
Niska: 50 (NW)
Nisqually: 11, 44, 45, 47 (NW)
Nooksack: 11, 44, 47 (NW)
Nootka: see Nuu-chah-nulth
Norridgewock: 50 (NE)
North Carolina Algonkians: 54 (NE)
Northern Athabascan: 15–20, 41 (NW)
Northern Ojibwa: 25, 26, 40–41, 54 (NW); 37, 40, 48 (NE)
Northern Paiute: 24, 25, 31, 33, 34, 35, 50 (GB)
Northern Shoshone: 36, 37, 38, 39, 50 (GB)
Nottoway: 11, 23 (NE)
Ntlakyapmuk: see Thompson
Nugumiut: 29 (NW)
Nutka: see Nuu-chah-nulth
Nuu-chah-nulth: 5, 6, 10, 38–39 (NW)
Nuxalk: 11, 21, 36, 42, 45, 46 (NW)

Occaneechi: 11, 51, 52–53 (SE)
Oconee: 50 (SE)
Ofo: 11, 47, 53, 54, 55 (SE)
Ojibwa: 40–41 (NW); 8, 9, 10, 27, 28, 29, 40, 55 (PP); 8–11, 20, 32–37, 40, 41, 48, 54 (NE)
Okanagan: 53, 54, 55 (GB)
Okchai: 34 (SE)
Omaha: 8, 11, 39, 40, 45, 52, 53, 55 (PP)
Oneida: 11, 13, 19, 22, 23, 24, 26, 34, 38, 50 (NE)
Onondaga: 11, 19, 23, 24,

30, 38–39 (NE)
Opelousa: 47 (SE)
Oregon Penutian: 53 (NW)
Osage: 8, 11, 39, 40, 51, 52, 53 (PP)
Oto (Otoe): 8, 11, 40, 51, 52, 53, 54, 55 (PP)
Ottawa: 8, 11, 14, 17, 32, 36, 40, 41, 48, 49, 54 (NE)
Owens Valley Paiute: see Eastern Mono
Ozette: 11, 39 (NW)

Padlimiut: 29 (NW)
Padouca: 12 (SW)
Paiute: 11, 24, 25, 31–35, 37, 39, 40, 42, 43, 50. 52, 56 (GB); 6 (SW)
Pakana: 34 (SE)
Palouse: 11, 48, 53, 54 (GB)
Pamunkey: 57 (NE)
Panamint: 24, 25, 39, 41 (GB)
Papago: see Pima
Parklands People: 28 (PP)
Pascagoula: 11, 53 (SE)
Passamaquoddy: 11, 25, 27, 48, 50, 54, 55 (NE)
Patwin: 8, 56 (SW)
Paugusset: 55 (NE)
Pawnee: 8, 9, 10, 11, 12, 22, 38–39, 48, 50, 52 (PP); 15, 44 (NE)
Pawokti: 12 (SE)
Pawtucket (Pawtuxet): see Pennacook
Pecos Pueblo: 11, 34 (SW)
Pedee: 11, 53 (SE)
Pennacook (Pawtucket): 50, 51, 55 (NE)
Penobscot: 27, 50, 51 (NE)
Pensacola: 11, 53 (SE)
Pentlatch: see Puntlatch
Penutian: 26 (GB); 7, 22, 24, 56 (SW)
Peoria: 51, 52 (NE)
Pequawket: see Pigwacket
Pequot: 11, 43, 48, 50, 52, 55, 56 (NE)
Petun: 11, 16, 23 (NE)
Piankashaw: 52 (NE)
Picuris Pueblo: 40 (SW)

Piegan: 16, 18, 20 (PP)

Pigwacket: 50 (NE)

Pikuni: see Piegan

Pima and Papago: 9, 10, 11, 26–27, 46, 47 (SW)

Piscataway: see Conoy

Pit River: 35 (GB); 29, 50 (SW)

Plains Cree: 10, 25, 27–29 (PP)

Plains Ojibwa: 41 (NW); 9, 27, 28, 29, 55 (PP); 32 (NE)

Pocomoke: 56 (SE)

Pocomtuc (Pocumtuck): 48, 54, 56 (NE)

Podunk: 51 (NE)

Pojoaque Pueblo: 40 (SW)

Pokanoket: see Wampanoag

Pomo: 7, 8, 11, 23, 28–29, 55 (SW)

Ponca: 8, 11, 39, 40, 53, 55 (PP)

Potawatomi: 11, 40–41 (NE)

Powhatan: 11, 48, 56, 57 (NE)

Pueblo Dwellers: 33–45 (SW); 9, 34, 38, 54 (PP)

Puntlatch: 43, 44–45 (NW)

Puyallup: 11, 43, 44, 45, 47 (NW)

Qikirmiut: 30 (NW)

Quaitso: see Queets

Quapaw 53, 55, 56 (PP); 17 (NE)

Quechan: see Yuma

Queets: 45 (NW)

Quileute (Quillayute): 11, 52, 53, 55–56 (NW)

Quinault: 11, 21, 22, 42, 43, 45, 56 (NW)

Quinnipiac: 51 (NE)

Quiripi: 48, 51 (NE)

Rabbitskins: 28 (PP)

Rappahannock: 57 (NE)

Raritan: 12, 50 (NE)

Ree: see Arikara

River People: 26 (SW); 29 (PP)

Rocky Boy and United States Cree: 29 (PP)

Sac: see Fox

Sadlermiut: 30 (NW)

Sagdlir Miut: see Sadlermiut

Sahaptian (Shahaptian): 11, 26, 48, 54, 56 (GB); 8 (PP)

Sakonnet: 57 (NE)

Salina (Salinan): 53 (SW)

Salish: see Flathead

Salishan: 22, 23, 42, 45, 47, (NW); 10, 12, 50, 51, 52, 54, 55, 56, 57 (GB)

Samish: 11, 45, 47 (NW)

San Felipe Pueblo: 40 (SW)

San Ildefonso Pueblo: 40–41, 43 (SW)

San Juan Pueblo: 41 (SW)

Sandia Pueblo: 41 (SW)

Sanetch: see Songish

Sanpoil: 11, 51, 54 (GB)

Santa Ana Pueblo: 42 (SW)

Santa Clara Pueblo: front cover, 10, 34, 36, 42, 44 (SW)

Santee Sioux: 43, 45 (PP)

Santiam: 54 (NW); 53 (GB)

Santo Domingo Pueblo: 42 (SW)

Saponi: 11, 51, 52, 53, 54 (SE)

Sara: see Cheraw

Sarsi (Sarcee): 11, 29, 56, 57 (PP)

Sauk: see Fox

Saulteaux: 25, 26, 40, 41 (NW); 27, 55 (PP); 32, 36 (NE)

Seechelt: 43, 45 (NW)

Sekani: 11, 19 (NW)

Semiahmoo: 11, 47 (NW)

Seminole: 8, 10, 11, 18, 34, 35, 39, 42–45, 46, 48, 49, 50, 53, 54, 57 (SE)

Seneca: front cover, 2, 14, 19, 22, 23, 24, 25, 38, 39, 49 (NE)

Senijextee: 51 (GB)

Serrano: 11, 50, 52, 53–54, 55 (SW)

Shahaptian: see Sahaptian

Shasta: 56 (NW); 7, 11, 54 (SW)

Shawnee: 24, (NW); 11, 14, 48–49, 59 (NE); 15, 19,

34 (SE)

Shinnecock: 53 (NE)

Shoshone: 6, 11, 26, 31, 35, 36–41, 43, 45, 50 (GB); 7, 8, 9, 12, 16, 22, 25, 26, 32 (PP)

Shoshonean: 6, 25, 31, 37, 39, 42 (GB); 33, 44 (SW); 25 (PP)

Shuman: 56 (PP)

Shuswap: 11, 12, 22, 52, 55 (GB)

Sia Pueblo: see Zia

Sikosuilarmiut: 29 (NW)

Siletz: 11, 12, 13, 14, 15, 45–46, 53, 54, 57 (NW); 54 (SW)

Sinkaietk: see Okanagan

Sinkiuse: 11, 50, 51, 53, 55 (GB)

Sinkyone: 11, 14 (NW)

Siouan: 8, 14, 30, 36, 40, 50, 51, 52, 53, 54, 55 (PP); 57 (NE); 7, 14, 47, 49, 51, 52, 53, 56 (SE)

Sioux: 28, 35, (GB); 8, 9, 10, 11, 21, 22, 23, 33, 34, 40–49 (PP); 32 (NE)

Sisseton Sioux: 11, 42, 43, 45 (PP)

Sissipahaw: 11, 49, 54 (SE)

Siuslaw: 53, 57 (NW)

Skagit, Upper and Lower: 11, 46, 47 (NW)

Skilloot: 11, 23 (NW)

Skitswish: see Coeur d'Alene

Skokomish: see Snoqualmie

Skykomish: see Snoqualmie

Smith River: see Tolowa

Snake: 16 (PP)

Snohomish: 11, 46, 47 (NW)

Snonowas: see Nanaimo

Snoqualmie: 11, 42, 44, 46, 47, 52 (NW)

Songish: 43, 46, 47 (NW)

Southern Paiute: 31, 32, 33, 34, 35, 42, 43 (GB)

Spokan (Spokane): 11, 12, 20, 26, 50, 51, 54, 55, 56 (GB)

Squamish: 11, 46 (NW)

Squaxon (Squaxin): 47 (NW)

Stalo: 11, 43 (NW)

Stillaguamish: 47 (NW)

Stockbridge: 11, 14, 26, 57 (NE)

Stoney: see Assiniboine

Straits: see Songish

Summerville: 41, 48, 49 (SE)

Suquamish: 11, 44, 47 (NW)

Susquehannock: 11, 23, 50, 56 (NE)

Swampy Cree: see West Main Cree

Swinomish: 11, 47 (NW)

Taensa (Natchez): 6, 11, 27, 29, 39, 40–41, 54, 55 (SE)

Tagish: 11, 17, 20 (NW)

Tahagmiut: 30 (NW)

Tahltan: 11, 17, 20 (NW)

Takelma: 11, 56 (NW)

Taltushtuntude: 11, 14 (NW)

Tamali (Tamathli): 50 (SE)

Tanacross: 19 (NW)

Tanaina: 11, 19–20 (NW)

Tanana: 11, 18, 19 (NW)

Taos Pueblo: 8, 38, 42–43, 45 (SW)

Tarramiut: see Tahagmiut

Tawakoni: 11, 57 (PP)

Tenino: 52 (NW); 11, 54, 56 (GB)

Tesuque Pueblo: 40, 43 (SW)

Tête de Boule: 11, 26 (NW)

Teton Sioux: 11, 41, 43, 45 (PP)

Thompson: 19 (NW); 56 (GB)

Tillamook: 11, 47 (NW)

Timucua: 54–55 (SE)

Tinde: see Jicarilla Apache

Tionontati: see Petun

Tiou: 55 (SE)

Tipai: see Diegueño

Tlingit: 6, 10, 11, 12, 17, 19, 20, 28, 48–49, 50, 51, 52, 53 (NW)

Tobacco Nation: see Petun

Tohome: 52 (SE)

Tolowa: 12, 14, 15 (NW)

Tonkawa: 11, 16 (SW)

Touchwood Hills: 28 (PP)

Tsimshian: 6, 11, 28, 50 (NW)

ABOUT THE CONTRIBUTORS

Richard Hook (Illustrator and Contributing Author)
An internationally respected professional illustrator specializing in historical and anthropological subjects for more than thirty years, Hook has had a lifelong interest in Native American culture that has inspired his remarkable artwork. He has been widely published in the United States, Europe, and Japan. A lifelong interest in Native American culture led to his selection as illustrator for the Denali Press Award-winning *The Enyclopedia of Native American Tribes*.

Michael G. Johnson (Author)
Johnson has researched the material culture, demography, and linguistic relationships of Native American peoples for more than thirty years, through academic institutions in North America and Europe and during numerous field studies conducted with the cooperation and hospitality of many Native American communities. He has published a number of books, in particular the Denali Press Award-winning *Encyclopedia of Native American Tribes*.